BUT WHEN YOU ARE OLDER . . .

# BUT WHEN YOU ARE OLDER . . .

## Reflections on Coming to Age

*Donald X. Burt, O.S.A.*

*A Liturgical Press Book*

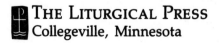

THE LITURGICAL PRESS
Collegeville, Minnesota

Cover design by Mary Jo Pauly

1     2     3     4     5     6     7     8     9

Library of Congress Cataloging-in-Publication Data

Burt, Donald X.
    But when you are older—: reflections on coming to age /
Donald X. Burt.
        p.  cm.
    ISBN 0-8146-2030-2
    1. Aging—Religious aspects—Christianity.  2. Christian life—
Catholic authors.  3. Aged—Religious life.  4. Augustine, Saint,
Bishop of Hippo—Views on aging.   I. Title.
BV4580.B87   1992
    248.8'5—dc20                                    91-46798
                                                          CIP

# Contents

# A Note on Sources

All citations in this book are either from the works of St. Augustine or from Sacred Scripture. Unless otherwise noted the translations of Augustine are my own and the translations of Scripture are from the New American Bible. To save space I have abbreviated references to the works of Augustine and have included them in the text. They are abbreviated as follows:

DCD   *De civitate dei* (The City of God)
DCR   *De catechizandis rudibus* (On Catechizing the Uninstructed)
DDQ   *De diversis quaestionibus 83* (On 83 Diverse Questions)
DDM   *De musica* (On Music)
DO    *De ordine* (On Order)
DVR   *De vera religione* (On the True Religion)
E     *Epistolae* (Letters)
ENN   *Enarrationes in psalmos* (Commentaries on the Psalms)
OIJ   *Opus imperfectum contra Julianum* (Incomplete Work Against Julian.)
S     *Sermones* (Sermons)

## Introduction: "To Live Until I Die"

The cliche which says "You are not getting older; you are getting better" is hopeful but unrealistic. The first part is a simple lie; the second part is a possibility. Like it or not, we *are* getting older and nothing can be done about it. Even if we sincerely deny it, we age just as fast. Like the person who plummets from the Empire State Building with the sincere conviction that he or she can fly, our sincerity in denying our age does not stop our jumping to a conclusion, nor does it slow the rate of acceleration. Like it or not, we are all getting older; and there is no use in exploring ways of stopping the process.

But it is fruitful to think about how to make it a positive process. It could just be the case that we indeed get "better" as we get older. Certainly our faith tells us that we are moving towards the "better" that awaits us beyond death, but even in this life our aging can bring progress. Our bodies may indeed be wearing out as we grow old, but we can increase in wisdom. We can learn from our history how to face up to our present and how to look to the future realistically.

Being realistic is the key. I am now in my seventh decade. Since I am neither a tortoise nor a redwood tree, I must reasonably assume that three-fourths or more of my life *on* the earth is over and my time *under* the earth is fast approaching. After a career of *looking over* various parts of this world, I will soon be *overlooking* Philadelphia from that

hilly cemetery where all good Villanova Augustinians wait
for resurrection.

There is no use in dreaming impossible dreams about
the rest of my life on earth. My chances of finally becoming a basketball star are over and done with. I jump now
only from the waist up. I will never be able to marry my
eighth-grade love. Having rejected me in my prime it is unlikely that she would be attracted by my fossilized physique
unless she is even more debilitated than I. I no longer have
the time to become a brain-surgeon. Having taught philosophy for thirty or more years, a philosopher I will remain
as my Being becomes Non-Being and my Matter loses all
Form.

There is no use "mooning" over what was or what might
have been. My happiness is determined by my present and
my future and these are the realities I must deal with. As
St. Augustine says: "Nothing is so hostile to hope as to look
back, to place hope in those things which flit by and pass
away. We must place our hope in those things which are
not yet given and will be given in our future . . . especially
those things which are unchanging" (S 105, 5.7).

But what *is* there to look forward to when you are old?
When he was seventy-two, Augustine wrote to a friend that
there was no use in him (Augustine) hoping for another age
in this life (E 213, 1). His point was that when we are old
we cannot say: 'Well, when I get to the next stage of my
life, everything will work out just fine." What we have is
what we will have in this life. Certainly we can look forward (as Augustine did) with great joy and relief to those
days beyond death when everything will be "just fine" forever, but in the meantime we must deal with the life we have
now.

And so it is with me. Like an old oak, my days of being
ten and being twenty and being thirty and being forty and
being fifty are all there underneath my sixty-year-old outer
layer, but I cannot go inside and relive those days without

destroying the life that I have, the life of a somewhat gnarled and scarred but nevertheless impressive tree. My trunk has broadened in base and my roots are beginning to show. I am no longer a sleek sapling growing from one narrow piece of land. Over the years I have branched out somewhat irregularly into unexpected spaces. My history casts shadows now where others may rest and perhaps learn. I have been filled out by the vines of love that cling to me. To attempt to prune away the ages and return to past days would only make me into a poor old stick, bereft of that foliage which has come to define my being. And this would be sad. Much better by far to be "old Don" than "wan Don."

There may even be some benefits in being "old Don." A long time ago a teacher told me that metaphysics does not begin to make sense until you are sixty. That is an interesting prospect. Metaphysics is said to be the science of Being and thus a master metaphysician should be a master of existing. Supposedly she or he has acquired the virtue of wisdom, the ability to look at life and "put it all together." Now that I am sixty, perhaps I have a chance to make some sense out of this thing called human life. Perhaps I have moved beyond aerobics and am on the verge of metaphysics. I have stopped jogging in circles and am about to settle on a definite direction in life. Just in time! I am somewhat out of control physically and mentally. My belly lops over my belt and my dreams lop over my logic.

My dominant dream just now is to truly *live* until I die and then die unafraid. This is my dream and my hope and my prayer. The purpose of this book is to think about how these goals can be accomplished. How indeed can I live each of my days this side of death as fully as possible, with no days terribly diminished by boredom or guilt or fear or pain?

It is an important question for any of us who are "long in the tooth" (and indeed for those who are still "teething"). Sometimes as death approaches we humans give up on living. Sometimes when a love is lost by death or separation we humans pack in the rest of our lives and withdraw into morose isolation. Sometimes when we humans are forced to do the same things day after day—the same old jobs repeated again and again—our spirit becomes paralyzed by boredom and the good things in life become dulled and grey. And then we die, passing out of this earth's daylight as we entered—with a whimper. None of us want that. We want to live fully and completely every moment of this life. We want to live until we die.

The achievement of that goal depends partially on whether we can face death with equanimity. Death is a fact and should not be ignored, but neither should it come to dominate our lives. We should not spend every moment of our lives worrying about death lest we forget how to live. We should not come to feel that our life is of no importance because we shall someday die. We should not cease to be excited about today and even anticipate tomorrow just because some tomorrow will be our last today. We can't do anything about the fact of death. But we can face that fact and try to make the best of it. We can even try to make it an instrument of happiness, an instrument that will cause us to value even more this day that we have now. We must think about death now courageously and wisely if we are to live authentically today. To live as though we were not to die is to live in fantasy. To live fearing death exorbitantly is to eviscerate this moment of life that is still ours.

I want to live until I die and then die unafraid. Thus I must speak to myself now about the reality of my life, trying to understand it, seeing it as it is with its fullness and its emptiness.

I must speak to myself about my present age and try to respond to it authentically—as a human with mind and heart and hope and faith in Jesus Christ. Augustine tells me that I am indeed "old" when I reach sixty, but that this final stage of life can last as long as all my other ages put together (DDQ 83, 58.2). I could live many years as an old man.

It is important that I try to understand and accept what is going on inside me—in my body and my spirit.

My God friend Jesus tells me much about living and dying. So does my human friend Augustine. Perhaps by reflecting on their words, I can find more meaning in my present age. Perhaps in reflecting on their lives, I can face my own death with equanimity.

It is worth a try.

# Images of Life: The Golden Years　1

A dear friend of mine, now bent by the disability of her ninety years, once said to me that "the Golden Years are not what they were cracked up to be."

And so it is. Few of us are destined to look or run about like those beautiful seniors in *Modern Maturity*. This is not surprising. Fact falls short of fantasy at every age. As I remember it, when I was a kid none of my ruffian pals had the well-scrubbed innocence of those pictured in *Boys World*. In my later wanderings through the alleys of Philadelphia, I found few *Cosmopolitan* women or *Esquire* men. The fantasy of such magazines is not bad as long as we do not take it seriously, as long as we do not feel cheated when our reality falls short of fantasy's perfection.

Now that I am in my sixties, I must face the prospect that my years of gold may not be all that they "have been cracked up to be." But it should not surprise me. Augustine tells me: "We have all been put into the furnace and we have all come out of it a little bit cracked" (ENN 99, 8). I have been a cracked pot from my first day out of the kiln, and all of my ages have been cracked since, always a bit off-center from perfection.

Now that I am in my golden years, I have come to see that each of my ages tested my metal as a person and each had its own special metallic sheen.

My first years were days of filmy silver. I was like a precious spider-web, something to be enjoyed but not taken

15

seriously. Recently escaped from nothingness, I was still almost nothing—a new being in desperate need of nourishment and shaping. I was a minor matter with little form.

My teens were brassy times. Newly discovering the world, I questioned all advice from those who had gone before. Their words were just too outdated for application to a spirit as young and bright as mine. I was loud and proud but scared inside.

My twenties were my age of mercury. I could not be captured by any place. Young and vital and bright, I was always on the move. I had vim and vigor and the certainty that the next event would always be exciting and full of laughter.

My thirties were my copper years, more pliable than my days of brass yet more stable than my mercurial "twenties." I was able now to accommodate a bit to the views of others. I no longer flitted. My life had a sheen to it, and I was conscious that it contained something good. I had become a conduit through which things of value passed to others. I had become a "solid citizen," a stable member of the human race.

My forties were my age of steel. I prided myself on being a tower of strength to those who needed help, a problem-solver with (supposedly) no problems to be solved. I did important jobs and was secure in my loves and planned second and third careers after my present jobs were done.

In my fifties my supposed steel turned out to be iron. I began to rust. My outside needed more frequent grooming to be presentable. My inside needed more courage to face my increasing deterioration. I was still a point of security for others but now a rusty haven. They came to me for my experience and no longer for my "new ideas." I became a source of nostalgia, a tale-teller difficult to turn off.

Each of these earlier ages had its own fear and its own unfulfilled desire. When I was four, I longed to be eight so that I could cross the street and find happiness in some Eden on the next block. When I was eight, I longed to be sixteen and drive to more distant Edens (e.g., Wildwood, New Jersey) where I could have a continuing "blast" with friends who liked me and took me seriously. When I was sixteen, I dreamed of being twenty-five and being independent, making my Eden with my own hands and finding an Eve who would not only take me seriously but even love me. When I was twenty-five, I dreamed of being thirty and being settled in my life, beyond the danger of mistakes about the Eden I would choose and the Eve to whom I would give my life. But when I was thirty, I found myself trying to act like twenty and paying the price in liniment and bandages and the hidden smiles of those who recognized a fool. Reaching forty, I ceased speaking about age altogether but rejoiced secretly when others said I looked like thirty. When I was fifty, I realized that the days of starting over were over. What I was was what I would be. Now that I am sixty, I forget how it was to be forty, and I worry about how I shall be at seventy. And, when finally I am seventy, I will probably get up in the morning and be pleased with that modest victory.

Indeed my Golden Years may not be perfectly golden, but what else is new? Continuing to live through these imperfect years is certainly better than the alternative. And it is better than "going back" and growing up again. Augustine once said that he would prefer to die rather than be a child again (DCD, 21.14; 22.22). I think I agree with him. I am too long for short pants and too broad for knickers.

Now that I am up and about for another one of my "golden days," I might as well get on with it. I do not feel any radically new pains, most joints seem to be working, and I hear the clicking of at least a *few* brain cells. Let me grab hold of this golden day with all of its imperfection and sit back and watch my sunset.

# "But When You Are Older . . ."   2

**A** short while before he visibly left this earth, Jesus turned to his friend, Peter, and said: "I tell you solemnly: as a young man you fastened your belt and went about as you pleased; but when you are older you will stretch out your hands, and another will tie you fast and carry you off against your will" (John 21:18).

Four hundred years later the old Augustine read the passage and made the laconic comment: ". . . and so it is when you grow old" (S 335B, 3).

Of course, when Christ was speaking to Peter, he was predicting his crucifixion, not how he would be as an old man. But he could just as well have addressed the words to John, the only apostle that died a "natural" death at an advanced age. There is a tradition that at the very end John had to be carried about from place to place by his friends and his conversation was restricted to saying only one thing: "Little children, love one another!" It was a valuable message and (being a saint) John was probably not bothered by his incapacity, but I suspect that there were a few who saw him and said: "What a sad state for poor old John to come to. He who was called a 'Son of Thunder,' has in the end become a 'Child of the Mist.'"

Now that I have come to age, I understand that Christ's prophecy for Peter is also a prophecy of what may happen to EVERYMAN if they live to be very old. It may indeed happen to me. It is a fearful prospect for one who has spent a life-time fighting to be "in control" of life: training the body to respond energetically to every wish, training the mind to analyze clearly and judge wisely in every situation. It is a terrible thing to face the prospect that the day will come when I must depend on others to take care of my most humble bodily needs, that I will need others to feed me and clean me and take me from here to there.

Of course, if I am unconscious, I will not be bothered by my disability as long as I am not in pain. I will have lost my sense of pride along with my ability to make sense. But *before* that happens, as I perceive the gradual dimming of mental faculties, I may experience an even greater sorrow—the sorrow that comes from knowing that the day is coming when I will be in time but not know what time it is, when I will not know who I am or where I am or whether I am loved. If my destiny is to spend my last days with a body out of control and a mind dim to the world, I indeed will realize the prophecy: "But when you are older . . . you will be tied fast . . . and be carried off against your will."

Of course, it may not happen this way. I may age gracefully, in full possession of my faculties. Indeed, since I was always slow of foot, my tennis game may not even suffer in my "old codger" period. But since there is the possibility that this will not happen, I need to face the prospect of "being bound" and make sense of it while I still have some sense.

There is certainly one truth that I can begin with: I indeed have *never* been free at any stage of my life. I seemed to be constantly *compelled* to do this and that by internal pressures that I could not control: the pressure to succeed, the pressure to be liked, the pressure to "make" something of my life. I wanted to love and be loved and, when it happened, found that I was not only "tied down" but also "tied up in knots" by the new experience.

If the truth must be told, now that I have come to age I sense more freedom than I ever had before. I no longer feel "driven" to succeed (I have pretty much done what I am capable of doing). My loves are settled: no new one's likely to occur; old one's pretty much in place with no "great expectations" from me. What a shame, at such a point in life, to have to suffer the pains of growing old! Just when I seem ready to use all my powers most effectively, they begin to fail me. Who can make sense of that?

Perhaps the prophecy of Christ to Peter can be of some

help. Peter was a strong man, impulsive, full of life, just given an important job. He had the love of a wife and the affection of good friends. At the precise moment when he was full of life, Christ called him to face his death. He called Peter to martyrdom—the most important act in his vigorous life. It was not Peter's living that confirmed his salvation. It was his acceptance of his dying, his acceptance of "being bound and carried away against his will."

Perhaps dying "being bound" by the disability of age is a martyrdom too. In a way "being a martyr" is nothing more than dying in and with Christ. Perhaps the only difference between being "crucified upside down" and dying with the disability of age is only in the length of time it takes. Perhaps the only difference between the deaths of the still vigorous Peter and the doddering old John was that, unlike their race on Easter Sunday, this time Peter got to the tomb first.

If it is the Lord's destiny for us, dying with disability is just as valuable as dying on a cross. In both cases he calls us to give up this life for the sake of something greater.

I hope that radical disability does not come to me. I hope I die at ninety-five just after a straight set victory over a scoffing youngster. But if that is not to be, I hope I remember that my final disability is just the way God has chosen to "tie me fast" before he takes me to a place "I could not choose" because it is beyond my imagination.

## *Old Love*                                      3

If you have any sense, your love becomes more precious as you grow older. You come to appreciate their loveliness more the longer you know them. You discover more things to love in them, not the least being that they have put up with you for so many years.

Some scoffers may say that you and your love are not as pretty as you once were but you know better. And it is not because your eyesight is failing. Admittedly, your eyes have gotten weaker over the years but your vision has gotten stronger. Now that you are older you can glimpse forever.

It should not distress you that your love has matured. Why would you want your love to be like those stringy young "Barbi" dolls and "Hulks" pictured in adolescent magazines? Older folk need loves of more substance— someone to "live with," not "work out with." A few extra pounds in a love gives more to hang onto as your years lengthen. The young are simply too angular and hard to embrace with enthusiasm. Like trying to hug a Nautilus machine, one must be careful not to be cut by the sharp edges of the young. Once you get older you prefer a few crevices in your love, even a crevasse or two to remind you of the scary times you have survived, a few crinkles around the eyes to remind you of laughter you have shared. The young are *too smooth* to be interesting.

An old love by your side is a constant reminder of the joy that comes from shared existence. You have *survived!* You have enjoyed years of ordinary comfortable days. Here and there were moments of ecstasy, but mostly the days were times when nothing much seemed to be happening but were yet warmed by awareness of another who cared that you existed.

You have survived moments of self-doubt, wondering whether you loved with too much passion or too much selfishness. You have survived the fear of losing your love because they finally discovered how blemished you were. You have experienced the relief of realizing that indeed they *do* know you as you are and care for you none the less. Now you can sit back and *know* the truth of Augustine's words:

"Caring and cared for, each drop of time becomes precious to me" (C, 11.2).

Old loves are better because they long ago gave up hope (if they ever had it) that you would be a world-conqueror or anything of great moment. They have given up hope of "changing you" and instead have filled up your gaps with their fullness. They have taken your mediocrity and christened it "Excellence" by their love.

It has lasted, your old love, and has given you reason to believe (and no longer just hope) that it will indeed accomplish that innocent promise made when first you met: "Our love shall be forever." And so it shall be, because it is *old* love. Having lasted through time, it just *must* be eternal. You just *know for sure* that when that time beyond time comes you shall be together forever.

You can't be together forever just now. Life gets in the way and death is still to come. Some separation is inevitable. But old love can stand even that. It does not depend on its beloved being here and now present. Over time the beloved comes to live in your memory and imagination and you can always touch them with your heart. Their lovely spirit casts an aroma that surrounds you wheresoever you go. Anytime you wish you can reach out to your old love with the fingers of your day-dreams and caress them.

Certainly it is no substitute for a good solid squeeze, but it is enough to carry you through until the day comes when you can again hold in your arms the one you have so loved for such a long, long time.

So all things considered, old love is not a bad thing at all. In truth it is the *only* thing possible for you when you wake up one day and find that you are old but still very, very much in love.

## *The Peace of Limits*  4

There is a fine prayer that I have come to understand now that I have come of age. It is from the Book of Psalms and is a short, joyful prayer of a human being who has found peace in limits. I imagine that the psalmist was a bit "long in the tooth" when he sang this song. Perhaps that is why it is so short; ancients have little breath to waste on long ballads. In any case, it is a nice song and reflects how I feel some days—sitting by an open window watching others trying to climb the clouds. As I sit I sing softly:

> O Lord, my heart is not proud,
>   nor are my eyes haughty;
> I busy not myself with great things,
>   nor with things too sublime for me.
> Nay rather, I have stilled and quieted
>   my soul like a weaned child.
> Like a weaned child on its mother's lap,
>   so is my soul within me (Ps 131:1-2).

The song reflects the stillness and quiet that can come with age—the quiet of the old man sitting on a bench watching the present and remembering the past, the stillness of the long-married couple strolling by the sea, holding hands, joined in a love that no longer needs many words.

The limits that come with age can be a peaceful release. New ventures are precluded by lack of time and energy. Others have ceased to have grandiose expectations of us. We are no longer their "problem-solver" (though we may be considered their "problem"). No one expects us to run a marathon or start a new career or have a new family. We can walk now and need not run. We have become whatever we at an earlier time could come to be. If we have had kids, they are grown and on their own. They are responsible for themselves and no longer can we be forbidden the delicious excuse: "So they *are* crazy! But don't blame me!"

We no longer need to build new castles in this world. We have turned that last corner and can now spend our days idly cleaning up loose ends on projects started long ago, pulling them together so that we can sit back and rest.

Now we sing the final stanza of the song that is our life— a providential rhythm which dictates that each of us enters the course of time quietly, gradually grows in strength, makes our mark, and then sits back and watches a new age take over the reins of power. In these last quiet days the time for delusions of grandeur are over. If people are to love us now, they must love us for what we *are* for them rather than for what we can *do* for them.

Our souls are stilled and quiet, finally weaned from the passion to be more than we are, from the pretence of being more than we could ever be. We sit still in the embrace of God's providence, like a weaned child on its mother's lap. We stop shouting at the world about this and that and sit quietly in the lap of God and hear his whispered words:

> Can a woman forget her infant,
>    be without tenderness for the child of her womb?
> Even should she forget,
>    I will never forget you.
> See, upon the palms of my hands I have written your name
> (Isa 49:15-16)

It is true that in my age I have returned to the limits of my infancy, but with an important difference. Now I know where I am and where I have come from and where I can go. My limits give me time to think about all these grand things.

I have achieved the young Augustine's desire to know some thing about self and something about God (DO, 2.18). Now that I have come of age, I have come to see the limits of my self, and beyond those limits I have found the protecting arms of God. I sit quietly and am at peace.

## *The Joy of Remembering*                                5

**B**eing old is like sitting on a tall hill and looking back over the valleys of my life. Sitting there I can focus my memory on any garden of delight and revisit familiar places and dear departed loves. Looking back I can see how each part of my past fits into the pattern of my life. When my past was present, I could not get perspective and I missed much of the beauty. To use Augustine's analogy, I was like a person concentrating attention on one small tile in a mosaic floor, too busy burying my nose in this little piece of space to see the glorious beauty of the whole (DO, 1.1.). So too when I was younger I was often so consumed in the pleasure and pain of a little piece of my time that I could not make sense of it. I had too little past to understand my present.

In memory all lovely times and places, all lovely events and lovely people, become forever part of my being, ready to be called back and caressed at any moment. In memory the narrow little world of "me" expands to fullness. I embrace and contain the whole world of my history, and from those remembrances I fly to worlds that never were. My remembrances supply the raw material for my imaginings. My memory is the foundation for my identity. Without memory I could never dream. Without memory I would lose myself. Indeed, as Augustine remarked: "In memory I meet myself" (C, 10.8). Sometimes it seems that when a person grows very old, their contact with the present softens. But this is so only because the world of memory is coming into sharp focus. They seem to forget about today and lose all fear of the future as they return again and again to events of their distant past. Sometimes long deceased loves become more real to them than the person who has just left their room. In my mother's last days she often confused me with my long dead father, but that was fine because it brought her joy. Indeed, on the brink of the next world, her dead husband was probably closer to her than her living son. Some said that she was in a sorry state, but the sorrow was only in the hearts of the loved ones who were forgotten even as they stood by her side.

Now that I am older I can understand her last days better. I find myself living in the past more and more, sifting through the files of memory examining all my years, good and bad, trying to make sense of them, trying to enjoy again the moments of joy, trying to erase moments of foolishness or perversity or weakness or malice, trying to edit out (or at least diminish) those bad times which have scarred and wounded my heart or the hearts of those I love.

I love especially to go back to one special year, a year that was a very good year. I like to pull it from my memory-bank and flash it unchanged on the screen of my imagination. I love to revisit its bright shining moments, to feel again the passion for life and love that then coursed through my veins, to feel again the peace of intimate conversations with friends, to *be* again what I was then. As I wander the past shores of those pleasant times, see again the blue sky and shining seas, smell again the aromas of its fragrant spring, feel again the hot passion of its summer, thrill again to the kaleidoscope of its autumn colors, feel again the brisk purity of its winter snows, I say to myself that "it was indeed a very good year."

Now that I am older my powers for present accomplishment may be somewhat diminished, but my life is even more full. I have *history* and I remember it with fondness. People may say that I am losing contact with reality, but in fact I am discovering its breadth. Now I have not only a present to be endured but also a past to be enjoyed, especially that magic time that was "my very good year."

# *Images of Life: The Merry-Go-Round* 6

By the time you are very old, you have gone through many funerals and you begin to wonder at the mystery of it all. It seems that death is all wrong in so many cases. Children die before their parents. The old and the sick linger on for years and years, outliving those strong, younger folks who had taken care of them. It is all so mixed up. Those who are very much prepared to "pack it all in" and get on with the next life linger on and on, experiencing the sadness of seeing all their friends and loved ones go before them. At the same time some youngsters are snapped up by death in the prime of life or even before their prime.

It seems so unfair! Once placed on the path of life we should be guaranteed a certain distance to make our mark for time and eternity. When we have everything going for us—youth, energy, anticipation—our road should not suddenly come to an end. To be sure, every life must end finally in death and eternity, but we should be given a decent amount of time to have our run. And when finally we run out of steam, when we are obviously coming to the end of the road, it should not be necessary to crawl those last few yards inch by painful inch. The mystery of life is that some are close to death and cannot clutch it while others have life snatched away before they have a chance to even begin. How to make sense of it?

Much of the problem comes from a mistaken image of what our life is really like. As long as we see life as a straight path with conception at the beginning and eternity some place way off in our future, there is no explanation for the comings and goings of human beings. It will always seem that the young die out of due time and the very old linger beyond their due time. We will always be surprised when a youngster is snapped up by an eternity that should be so far down the line. We shall always agonize over the long-lived person who spends so many unpleasant years waiting at the door of the next life and being unable to get in.

The image of our life as a long straight path can lead us to much foolishness too. If we think that we are not very close to the end of our life (when finally we must come to account and pay our dues), we can come to believe that we are safe in doing pretty much what we please. The eternal, infinite world is so far ahead! Our Father is so far away! We have *plenty* of time to stake out our little space and to enjoy ourselves. We have time to enjoy the music. There is time enough later on to play the piper.

Now that I am older and remember the young who have died and the elderly who have lingered, I have come to realize that whatever our age we are all equally close to eternity. My life is not like the races I used to run on the long, broad beach at Wildwood, New Jersey. It is more like the rides I so loved on the Boardwalk merry-go-round.

It was a wonderful experience, those merry-go-round rides—whirling around and around midst the flashing lights and happy music. When I was very little (just beginning my life of riding), I was restricted to those stationary horses that did not move up or down. Such modest riding was exciting enough for me at the time. In those days of innocence, I did not need to scale new heights or experience new depths to get a kick out of life. It was quite enough for me to whirl around and around, pretending to cover great unknown spaces on my noble steed. The world beyond the merry-go-round seemed to fade away. It became a blur and I ceased to pay attention to my father, who stood but a few feet from my twirling life, ready to take me home when the ride was over. Reality for me became the merry-go-round and the people who shared with me my spinning world.

Stupid kid that I was, I did not think about the fact that my merry-go-round world was always encircled by Wildwood, New Jersey, no matter how long my journey lasted.

I did not think about the fact that my ride could end at any time and that then I would be called home by my father who waited just a few short steps away.

When I became older my merry-go-round life was lived with more style. I graduated to the horses that leaped up and down. Now I survived the depths and climbed to the heights, pretending that I was Lord of World. I took chances with life, sometimes riding with purpose like a jockey straining to win a race, and at others swinging wildly from the saddle like an acrobat as I grabbed at the elusive gold ring that was the sign of success in my whirling world. Comfortable with my exciting life, I looked around for someone to share it with me. I met new loves and I showed them all my tricks. I acted like a carousel king and I vowed that I would forever be the protector of any princess who would come ride with me.

Stupid man that I was, I forgot that no matter how far or how masterfully I rode, no matter how many gold rings I acquired, no matter how many princesses loved me, my merry-go-round world was always encircled by Wildwood, New Jersey. I did not think about the fact that my ride could end at any time and that then I would be called home by my Father who waited just a few short steps away.

In my later years I still enjoyed my merry-go-round ride, but now I sat with other old folks in those gaily decorated carriages sprinkled here and there among the leaping horses. My days for riding and catching gold rings and finding new princesses were over, but the happy music and the flashing lights were as good as ever and I got enjoyment from just sitting, watching the youngsters, and feeling the breeze of living in my face as I whirled on. I said to myself: "How pleasant it is to sit here on this merry-go-round and watch the rest of the world go by." I knew that my time was short, but I promised myself a few more rides of peace, enjoying old loves, reminiscing with friends about the good old days.

Stupid old codger that I was, I still found it hard to understand that no matter how far I had traveled, my merry-go-round world was still encircled by Wildwood, New Jersey. I found it hard to accept the fact that, no matter how good I felt, my ride could end at any time and that then I would be called home by my Father who waited just a few short steps away.

Now that I am older I have come to see that there is no good time to die nor bad time to die. There is only my time. I have come to see that, no matter how young or old I may be, no matter how long or short my ride may have been up to this moment, the world of my merry-go-round is still encircled by the infinite, eternal world of the Father who stands but a few steps away. At any moment my ride could be over and the Father will reach out, take my hand, help me down, and take me home with him.

In some strange way I am comforted by that thought, now that I have come of age.

## Pleasure in Surviving                                7

One of the pleasures of living to an extended age is being able to look back over the years and realize that you have survived without doing too much damage. You have lasted in your solemn vows; you have kept the faith; you have not hurt too many others and now there is little time left to mess up. You are close to the time when you will hear those wonderful words of the angel witnessing the happy horde trooping into the Heavenly City: "These are those who have lasted!" (cf. Rev 7:14).

Surviving is no mean accomplishment. A dying friend of mine told me that in his view the most difficult and important task in life is to avoid some horrendous "perverting" choice, a choice which irrevocably changes your life for the worse. He cited the case of a young man with a grand future ahead of him who ended all of his life by his decision to try drugs just once. There is no recourse from that first drug overdose. There is no recourse from that one perversity that destroys reputation. There is no recourse from that one infidelity that destroys a family. Life may go on after a perverting choice, but it is forever changed and saddened.

The worst perverting choice is that choice that makes a person turn away from God forever, but this is not always a loud, defiant rejection. Sometimes a "perverting choice" in this life so destroys us that we give up hope of forgiveness and descend into a black hole forever. We rush from heaven not with a curse but with a whimper. Our perversity can be forgiven by God, but we cannot forgive ourselves, and we doubt that any being who *could* forgive us could be God. Strangely enough our despair is rooted in pride; our sin is *too big* even for a *God* to handle.

The saving grace for the humble is to know that there is no bad choice that cannot be forgiven by God. The wisdom of the humble is to admit that they are bound to make *some* bad choices in the course of a lifetime. The fortitude of the humble is in their effort to avoid those bad choices which would *irreparably* wound themselves or others.

It is not an easy task. It can be accomplished only with the help of God and a bit of luck. When you are older you can look back and be thankful for the narrow escapes you have had. You can be thankful but you must not take credit for your escape. For example, Augustine advises that if you are tempted to pride because you never became an adulterer, you should listen to God saying:

> You were not an adulterer because I preserved you. At times I saw to it that you had no willing companion. At other times I saw to it that there was no time or place to do it. And when finally you had the time and the place and a pres-

ent willing companion, I scared you so effectively that you did not have the gumption to go through with it (S 99, 6.6).

Augustine suggests that when you look back at a somewhat imperfect life and realize how many times you came close to disaster, you should begin praising God for the sins you did *not* commit.

No matter how old we get there is no room for complacency. We can never say that "I now have my house in order. There is no danger that I will ever again make a silly decision." Augustine was much impressed (but not surprised) by the story of a man who, after living virtuously with his wife for twenty-five years, suddenly kicked up his heels at the ripe old age of eighty-three and took up with a young lyre girl (OIJ, 3.20). She was musically inclined, but he was given to more primitive inclinations; and his being in his ninth decade did not seem to dampen the fires of his lust too much.

Who knows? Perhaps hearing that story was a final grace for Augustine. A few years later when he came to die, the seventy-four-year-old bishop had the penitential psalms painted in big print on the walls of his sick room. He wanted to be able to see them till the very end and praise God for protecting him from past disaster. He also wanted to remember to keep up his prayers. Recognizing his past stupidity, he knew that without the help of God there was still a chance for him to fall into a terrible "perverting" choice that could warp his eternal future. Augustine *remembered* what he was like, prayed for help, and *survived* till the very end.

## Slowing Up and Cooling Down          8

Now that I have come of age, I notice that I am gradually slowing up and cooling down. It was not so in the days of my youth. Then I seemed to be always running, pushed by a caffeine jag that kept every nerve sparking and twisting on the lookout for something new and exciting. My attention span then was short. I exhausted every event of content in a few moments and anxiously looked beyond it to anything that would rescue me from boredom. I would run and run and run with no fixed goal in mind—like a jogger endlessly going around and around the same track, anxiously timing himself to discover how long it took to go nowhere.

My days of such exercise are over. Now I plod along the path of my life passed by assorted youths running I know not where, to do I know not what. In my running days I was more concerned about keeping up than thinking about my running. It is only now that I have come of age, that I have time to sit back in my orthopedic chair, massage my aching knees, and wonder at frantic running of the young.

My perception now is that the young seem always to be running (even when they are walking). They run to "work out" (though they don't need to). They run to "party" (celebrating their stamina, I suppose). They run to eat fast-food so that they can run even faster. They pretend to be "cool," but to me they seem quite steamy—hot with excitement about so many things to do and so many events to experience. They seem ever to be in need of a cold shower. Their faces are flushed and their eyes are shining and their voices are very, very loud (especially at midnight on a college campus).

I am in accord with Augustine's view that given the choice between dying and growing up again it is better to die, but I do envy the young their innocent passions. In my present state I find it hard to work up a sweat about anything. I have heard most "great" speeches at least twice before, and great "causes" seem to differ only in the color of their flags. In the past I spent my passions on many words and many works, but now I need to ration my energies carefully. Any extravagant exercise havocs my blood pressure. Age has "cooled me down." Now I refuse to be upset by any human absurdity except my own. Now I horde my enthusiasm for the few works I can do well. Now I shepherd past loves rather than "being on the prowl" for someone new.

I like to believe that my present quiet state is a sign of tolerance and not indifference. I hope that my narrowed activity is more directed energy than simple lethargy. I hope that my slowing up and cooling down is a sign of coming to life rather than losing life. It may be that my rejection of frantic motion is bringing stability. It may be that I am beginning to achieve the dream of philosophers: moving from the *Many* to the *One*, gaining a simplicity of life that is the beginning of wisdom.

Augustine gives me some hope that my movement from the "fast track" has put me on the right track. In the midst of his own busy career, he spoke about the dangers of that "curiosity" which causes us to flit from one experience to another and makes us more interested in juicy gossip than gospel wisdom. He warns that such consuming petty concerns in the here and now stand in the way of seeing the God above or of preparing for the eternity yet to come (C, 10.35).

When we bury ourselves in the news of the day and the party of the moment, we are like runners racing around and around the same track. We run and run but do not know why and seem to have no time even to ask the question. Minds dulled by entrancing motion, we are powerless to step back and distinguish between the important and the unimportant. Indeed, "everything" seems important because it is "what's happening." We get so wound up by our constant motion that we are unable to think at all (DM, 6.13).

As I sit here I cannot deny that I am slowing up and cooling down. Trying to get up makes me face that fact. But this change in my life may not be all that bad. For one thing my knees do not ache as much as they did when I was a jogger, running after a shape I never had. And who knows? As I sit here exercising my spirit, I may be in a more important sort of "training program," preparing myself for the quiet contemplation of Love which (I am told) is the major activity in heaven. I am assured that my lack of speed will not stand in my way there. In the heavenly city there are no jogging tracks and there is no need to run. Even the slowest of us will have an eternity to get where we wish to be.

## *My Old Friend (my body)* 9

Augustine says that when I get to heaven I will be friends with my body (S 155, 14.15).

I certainly hope so. Now that I have come to age, it seems that most days are days of uneasy truce. And truly I am not consoled by my mentor's assurance that "you only grow old on the outside" (E 147, 2). It is precisely my *outside* that becomes an increasing *pain* as the years go by.

It was not always thus. I remember days when my body was truly a friend, merrily following along when I decided to run or swim or take a trip to foreign places. It stayed awake during the day and slept peacefully all night, never demanding that it be taken for a little walk in the wee hours of the morning. In the days of its youth, it allowed me to jog in shorts. Now it forces me to walk with short pants. Of course, it was troublesome at times, but because of an excess of life rather than a deficiency. It sometimes felt so good that it seemed to believe that it was invincible: able to party without penalty, able to add or shed pounds at will. So filled was it with the passions of youth, that sometimes it dragged my spirit into untoward places to do untoward things.

All that seems long, long ago now that I have come of age. My days of wine and roses are over; now I am in my nights of Maalox and frequent risings. Oh, my spirit may be getting younger, but my friend, my body, has definitely seen better days. This is the part that aches in bed in the morning, that is reluctant to get up, that forces me to sit quietly on the edge of my pallet before standing to make sure that all of us (feet and legs and torso and neck and all the rest) have gotten up together. My mind is awake and functioning at "dawn's early light," but all that is below is problematic. Before choosing daily underthings, my soul must check its recalcitrant underlings to be sure that they are ready for the challenge of getting dressed.

And so the day begins: a day with my spirit seeking wisdom and my body seeking a place to sit down, a day of avoiding mirrors, those shiny reflectors of past beauty now truly behind me, those silvered critics of the "outside" that I am now, those subtle prophesiers of what I shall be in the future. They say to my poor old body: "Despite the claims, there is no health club this side of heaven that can bring back your sweet bloom of youth."

But still I have friendly feelings toward my body. We have been together a long time now. Indeed, I do not know what I would do without it (and this is perhaps why death is still so frightening). As long as my body is not too disturbing, I am anxious not to be free of it. It is only through my body that I can smell the flowers and taste the bracing salt air and hear the sounds of birds and see the blue, blue skies and feel the gentle touch of one who cares for me.

Augustine assures me that my body, even decrepit, is good. It is indeed made in the image of God. There are traces of divine in my flesh and in tending to it carefully I am watering and pruning a temple of the Holy Ghost. Oh, it is true that God is more perfectly imaged in my spirit, and it is there that he primarily takes up residence. But the fact remains that I am not simply spirit; I am body and spirit, and if God loves me he loves me as I am. God may live in my spirit mostly, but only my old body can walk with him (as those first humans did once in Eden).

The pain that my old body feels some days is more a sign of what's right with it than what's wrong. It is fighting to stay together even as it falls apart. It seeks order even as it becomes more disorderly. The sometimes conflict between my spirit and my flesh is more like a lover's spat than an all-out war (S 155, 14.15). Indeed, the fact that it still *wants* to stand up in the morning is a sign of its nobility. As Augustine puts it:

> Although our body is like that of any other great beast in its dying and is weaker than many other's in its living, it still shouts of the goodness and the foresight of the Creator. Other animals are bent over towards the ground but we humans are made to walk upright looking at the heavens . . . . It makes you wonder at how great the soul must be considering how finely molded is its container, the body (DCD, 22.24).

If we are to believe tradition, Augustine did not have a very perfect body. He was plagued by one illness or another for most of his seventy-six years. Yet to his dying day he was convinced of this truth: when I stand before my morning mirror desperately searching for the "Donald that once was," if I look carefully I can see the handiwork of the God who *is*.

Some day my old body will be just fine. Even in his sixth decade of life (when he was already having problems getting his body up in the morning), Augustine could tell his friends: "Once this body is beyond its present corruption, once it is living that life beyond death. . . . My, oh my! how lightly will it leap and run! Anyone who tells you that you would be much happier without your old body is just *crazy!*" (S 141, 7.7).

As I sit here on this lovely morning, my spirit is overcome with joy at the thought of how fine my body shall be some day. Now, if I could only get my old friend to put on its socks.

## *My Body (cont.): Planned Obsolescence* 10

Still sitting here on the side of my bed, with one sock on and one sock off, I have finally realized what is happening to my old friend, my body. It is undergoing a process of planned obsolescence. I am becoming obsolete and it is in accord with a definite plan. I have contributed my sound to the symphony of time, and now I must pass on so that others may sing their unique notes.

All through my life I have complained about those cherished things that never seem to last: those shoes that just begin to fit at the very time when they must be destroyed for the sake of the environment; that favorite pair of cotton pants that begin to be molded to my frame at the very moment when they must be discarded for the sake of modesty; that wooden-shafted lady's four-wood with which I could do no wrong until that terrible day when it split in half giving its all to my last 250-yard drive; our 1929 family car that was the haven of my youth and worked just fine until its motor fell out on the streets of Philadelphia in 1943.

In each case the demise of the obsolete was a painful experience, but it was necessary to make room for the new: bigger and better shoes, wider and wider pants, new clubs that frequently gave me occasion for a good lie, and a sleek new 1944 Chevy coupe, which I was allowed to clean but not drive. Later on I learned that planned obsolescence is good for the economy and good for the soul. It is hard to get permanently attached to anything that is destined to wear out—things like my shoes and my pants and my toys and the family car and even (it seems) my old friend, my body.

As I sit here in the morning on the edge of my creaking bed (I have come not only to age but also to weight), contemplating my first great move of the day, I realize that my body too is becoming obsolete. Like it or not, my body is wearing out and wearing down. It is truly sad. If my old knock-about cotton pants were my friend, my old body is even a closer friend and it is sad to see it lose its sheen.

What makes the deterioration burdensome is that it is conscious. My spirit seems still young and it recognizes that it is trapped in a May–December marriage that is just not working out. And the distance seems to increase with age. As my body becomes more and more "lode-some" with its lowering bulk, more enervated, more hard of hearing and short of sight, my spirit seems to be getting more flighty and busy and perceptive. It is hard for my spirit to pay attention as my slow, old body lurches through its day. It is either running ahead of it in hope or running back to favorite past things or flying to the heavens in imagination.

Perhaps that is why I seem so often distracted, now that I have come to age. As my body sits stolidly on the side of the bed preparing for the challenge of the "second sock," my spirit flies hither and yon. It seems to sit in my body ". . . like a quiet child in its mother's lap" (Ps 131.2), dreaming of fantastic lands long forgotten by stolid adults. Now that I am older, I sit my obsoleting body on seashore benches, but my spirit whirls and dives with the gulls high above the distant sea.

My body is wearing out but this is according to plan. It *must* wear out to prepare for editions yet to come. It is true that I am literally running out of time, and all things of time are becoming obsolete for me; but I am running to eternity where shoes last forever and pants always fit and my drive will be long and true and my body will not need to wear socks ever again.

It is a grand prospect, but just now I must finish the time that is left to me. I must put on my sock, get up from the bed, and get on with the grand plan that is my life. I may be somewhat obsolete, but I am not dead—and there is much, much more life to come.

*Images of Life: A Life of Glass*     11

Augustine writes:

Are we not more brittle than if we were made of glass? Yet even though glass is brittle it lasts a long time if looked after. . . . But we humans, brittle as we are, are so subject to accidents in our lives that even though we may live through many threats of immediate destruction, we cannot survive for a very long time (S 17, 7.7).

Now that I am older, I have come to see the truth of his words. Now that I have come to age, I can see that my life all along has been a life of glass.

In the beginning I was whole and clear like a bell-jar blown into existence by the breath of God and in my infant years I rejoiced in such clarity. But as I grew I became frightened by such transparent existence, fearing that others would see through me and find only ugliness, or worse, something of no account at all. I began to cloud up my life with pretense, hiding myself from those around me and most of all from myself.

As I went through my life, there were times when I was hard and brittle, cutting others with my sharp edges. At other times I silvered myself over with possessions, making myself a mirror. When others sought me out, they saw only my surface—what I had or what I did or what I projected myself to be.

On my good days all my imperfections seemed to fade, and I was a clear window through which others could see the majesty of God. On my bad days, when I was warped and twisted by the heat of living, I gave distorted images of myself, the world, and those who looked at me.

Looking at myself now that I am older, I see that this glass life of mine is like ancient skin. It is no longer unblemished and uncluttered. Over time I have acquired a few marks, existence medals testifying to the good and bad that I have been through. Loves have scratched their initials on my surface and have pierced into my very heart. At times I have been cracked and even broken into shards by the vagaries of life. I am still alive, but now I live a life that resembles a kaleidoscope of shattered pieces stuck back together by the gentle love of those who care for me. Strangely enough, my life seems more rich. Now the light of the sun does not pass through me untouched but bursts apart into the colors of a rainbow, the white light shattered by the sharp edges of past wounds mended. I am no longer the simple person of my childhood. I have been marked by love. I carry the scratches of passing time. I may even be a more interesting window now.

On the other hand I may be just a pane.

*The Dark Side*      12

No book about getting old can be truthful if it ignores the "dark side" of the condition. To read some magazines for the elderly or to listen to some "experts" (usually in their thirties or forties) giving advice on growing old gracefully, you can come to believe that there are no problems in being old. But there are. The very old can suffer pains of body and pains of spirit that are difficult to bear and all the pious thoughts (some in this book) about being on the brink of eternity, all of the euphemisms about "golden years" and "senior citizenship" cannot take the pain away.

If we are unconscious of our condition, there is of course no pain for us—only for those who love us. But if we see what is happening to us, there can be great pain, a pain of anticipation if nothing else because we *know* that things will get worse, not better. We are distressed not only by what we have lost, but by what we will certainly lose. We suffer from the growing absences in our life.

It is hard to prepare ourselves for such absences. We don't think of what can go wrong when everything is going just right. We are not aware of our stomach until it begins to go bad. We don't value eight hours sleep until it is denied us. We sometimes take our loves for granted until we lose them. We don't realize the depth of our love for life until we become aware that we are dying. We ignore the good things in our life until we come to lose them. And once we lose them it is hard to remember how it felt to have them. We are like those lepers in the Gospel story (Luke 17: 12ff.) who forgot entirely about their healer once they lost their spots. Healthy, they forgot how it was to be sick; just as before, when they were sick, they could not imagine ever being healthy.

Sometimes the very old spend their days in silence because they cannot put their pain into words. We can speak about suffering only when we feel pretty good. I remember a friend of mine who had the habit of complaining "O, the pain!" when faced with day-by-day petty aggravations (like marking freshmen essays on a hot day). He used the phrase less frequently when he began to feel the disability of age. You don't joke about pain when it is present. Indeed, it would be somewhat redundant for your mouth to cry words of pain when your whole being mouths the reality.

The pains that come with age take various forms. On the physical level there may be the piercing pain of illness, but even without this blatant suffering there can be the suffering that comes from seeing one's body become more and more useless. The great athlete may in the end find it difficult to walk. The great manager may eventually find it impossible to manage even his own body functions. The great thinker may come to spend more time in forgetting than in knowing—sometimes standing perplexed in the middle of the room confused about where to go. The sage noted for quiet wisdom may in the end become quite garrulous—compelled, it would seem, to gabble all day about issues and places and events long since past. The great saviors who spent their lifetime carrying the weak and wounded on their backs, may come to depend entirely on others—others who must be *paid* to feed them and clean them and sit them by a window for a breath of air.

The pains of the old can also be pains of the spirit, pains that sometimes come from evaluating your past and understanding your present. If your past was glorious, there can be a sadness in realizing that your days of importance are over. Once you were a "mover and shaker" in the lives of others, there is now nothing to do but the trivial. Once you monopolized life; now you spend life playing Monopoly.

If your past was mediocre, that can be painful too. Looking back, you see only unrealized ideals, a life of accommodating principles to pressures, a half-life that cannot be amended. There is no time to start over, no time to find a new dedication or a new direction or a new love or a new anything. Your life has been a history of missed opportunities, and now it is too late to do anything about it.

When the dark days of my aging come, others may try to make me feel better but it is hard to find a way. Certainly cheerfully advising "Have a nice day!" will not do the trick.

If I *knew* how to make my day nice, don't you think I would do it without outside advice? I believe the saying of Simone Weil is very true: "No *other* human can share a person's private affliction." You may say to me, "I know just how you feel!" but you don't. My feeling is my feeling, not yours. Those who say to me "keep smiling" have not felt my pain. Those who say "have faith" have not experienced my forgetfulness. Those who say "have hope" have not felt my loss of control of life. Those who say "have charity" still have living loves who are close by.

Of course, there is an explanation for why these "dark" things happen when you get old. We feel bad because we want things to be so good. Even as it falls apart and loses control of itself, my poor old body still has its drive to be well "tied-together" and to live an orderly life. Even as it remembers its past indiscretions and foolishness and weakness, my spirit still has this dream of perfection: a life lived always at the peak of one's powers, a life that is of true importance, a life that is embraced by a perfect lover that will value me and never ever leave me alone.

Such explanation may indeed help me to *understand* my final condition. It is unlikely that it will make me *feel* any better. What will? It is hard to say. Perhaps the pain will not be so great if I have prepared for its possibility. Now when I still have a semblance of strength, now when I still have many enjoyable things in my life (some health, an interesting profession, some faithful loves), I must prepare myself to lose even them. I must accept the possibility that I will approach my final day on earth as naked and powerless as an unwanted embryo—bereft of consciousness, importance, and any semblance of human concern.

No matter how or when we die, we die naked, possessing nothing but ourselves. But Christianity teaches that no member of the human species is "junk," no matter how naked they may seem to be. There is always *One* who loves even the most "empty" of us.

Writing these words I think of a scene I witnessed some years ago. I was at the beach, sitting on the porch of a seashore house watching the world go by and feeling pretty good. A car parked in front of the house, and a young mother and father began the difficult process of lifting their terribly disabled son into a carriage so that they might take him for a little ride on the Boardwalk. It was sad to see and yet moving. The child was obviously cared for. Physically and mentally disabled, he was embraced by the love of those around him, even though he may not have been aware of it.

Faith teaches that even terribly disabled bodies encase eternal souls that will never be disabled. Disabled in time, such innocents will be saved for all eternity. Incapable of choosing against God in this life, God's choice of them is fixed forever.

Christianity teaches that just as that family lifted the body of their son from car to carriage so that he might see and smell the immensity of the sea, so God will lift us above our disability and carry us beyond this narrow life so that we might enjoy the sights and sounds that await just beyond the horizon.

I pray that, if I am unconscious at the end, God will lift me up anyway. I pray that, if am conscious, I will believe that it will happen. And if my emptiness stands in the way of such belief, I pray that the God who *IS* (despite my unbelief) will see me and say: "That's all right! He's not very *bad*. He's just very old."

## Belongings                                    13

As an old man Augustine remarked that one of the burdens of age is to outlive your loved ones. What he was saying was that when humans "come of age" they not infrequently lose all their belongings.

To have another human being belong to you is a precious gift. It means that you are the primary love in their lives. It means that they are ready and willing to drop everything else to be with you exclusively in heart and spirit and attention. It means that when you come to them for solace or for a few laughs, they do not say: "Just a minute, let me take this phone call first." It means that when you talk to them they truly *listen* to you rather than *putting up with* you until they can escape to more interesting endeavors. When another belongs to you, it means that they will turn off the television when you come into the room. It means that they will take your concern to heart immediately, rather than asking you to wait for the "beep" and then say your words into a mind which is "presently otherwise occupied but which will get back to you as soon as possible." When another belongs to you, it means that they have nothing more important in their lives at that moment than to be with you.

All of us (unless we are terribly unfortunate) have someone who belongs to us for at least part of our lives. Very few of us have such a treasure for every moment of our lives. Our loves have many loves themselves, and it is bound to happen that others—elderly parents, injured children, hurting friends—will have greater claim on their attention than we have at the moment. This yielding of our belonging to the needs of others can be borne if we are having a good day ourselves. We can busy ourselves about other things and wait our turn for attention from our loved one. While they go about their necessary business, we can bury ourselves in our job or devote ourselves to good causes or clean the house. Waiting our turn, we can take on the project of "getting in shape" (exercise and sports is often a grand narcotic for one who has lost their belonging). Doing a lot of things can distract us from the fact that for the time being at least we have no one who truly belongs to us.

However, if it is our destiny to achieve great age, it can become much more difficult to bear the feeling of "not belonging." This is especially so if one must live out one's last years as a widow or widower, having lost a long-loved spouse with whom one has shared a lifetime of mutual belonging. Their passing leaves a vacuum that no one else can fill. Even if one is surrounded by loving children and grandchildren, they cannot belong to you as your departed love did. They have other lives and other concerns and other belongings that must take priority in their lives. They are sorry for your trouble, to be sure, but they cannot always be with you in the midst of your need. They can't always be there to comfort you in your tears. They can't always be there to laugh with you when you are happy. It is no one's fault. It is just in the nature of things that some of us will outlive our belongings.

This being the case, it is important for us even before we come of age to try and develop that deep interior life that will allow us to live with solitariness if that is to be our destiny. To be solitary does not mean that we must be lonely. Being alone, even after a life of belonging, does not necessarily bring unhappiness.

If we have learned to live within ourselves, we can spend our time peacefully, remembering the lovely belongings we have had and looking forward to the day when we shall have them again in that heavenly land where there is no separation.

If we have learned to live a life of faith, we can understand that when all others are gone, we still belong to God and God belongs to us. We can come to know in the midst of our solitariness that this infinite God is the one belonging that we will never lose no matter how long we live—in time or eternity. We can *know* and be happy.

## *Old Passions*                                          14

When Augustine was in his forties, he wrote of the passions that he experienced as a youth of seventeen: "I was in love with the idea of love . . . I wanted to love and to have my love returned, and it would even be better if I could enjoy the body of my beloved. . . . I was also vain and ambitious, wanting to make my mark in the world" (C, 3.1). These were the passions of his youth, and they disrupted and to a certain extent dominated him over the next sixteen years.

When he was in his sixties, he admitted to his people that the battle still continued:

> "Even we who have grown old are still at war with our passions. They may have weakened, but they are still there. . . . We may dearly wish to get a little rest from such violent desires, but it is not within our power. Whether we like it or not, they tempt us and upset us and try to overcome us. You can try to suppress them; but can you do away with them? Never!" (S 128, 9.11).

His words are strangely encouraging to one, like me, who has come to age. Madness loves company even if misery does not, and it is somewhat comforting to know that when old angers come back and crazy ambitions arise and a passion for new loves burns in my sixty-year-old heart, this is just a sign that I am still a human—an *old* human but a human nonetheless.

The words of the elderly Augustine are also a warning to me that old passion can be just as destructive as the passions of my youth. Even worse, they can be downright silly. One can smile at the eccentricities of the young—falling in and out of love weekly, desperately trying to be "cool" in accordance with the fashion of the moment, dreaming of "making a lot of money" and thereby cutting a fine figure in the world. When the young are driven in this way, we only hope that they will survive the oats they are sowing. We can look upon them with a worried smile. But when the old indulge such passion, we laugh out loud and then cry a bit if we care for them.

It is natural for passions to be part of being old. It is silly to let them dominate one's life. It is silly because it is unrealistic. It is hard to say what prompts such elderly indulgence. Reasons are different for every person. For some, giving in to old passion is an attempt to convince oneself that the powers of youth have not been lost. Sometimes a missed adolescence is the cause. One either missed being silly in youth, or (even worse) now misses the silliness which one in fact enjoyed. For whatever reason silliness seems to build up in some over a lifetime, until finally the pressure gets too great and it explodes out of their now ancient container.

Silliness spews forth bringing amusement to strangers and pain to those who witness an old friend frantically trying to relive a past that never was. The effort is doomed from the beginning. Adolescent vigor has long since departed. Any missed loves are already occupied. There is no time to start a new career.

The passions of the old are not bad. Indeed, they bring fire into one's life. But the fires must be banked by a realization of what is possible and what is appropriate. One must be passionate about the good and evil in the world, one must be passionately in love with one's loves until the end of time (and indeed through eternity), but these passions should not lead to a time of silliness. To come of age means to accept one's age and sometimes dangerous passions that come with it.

We grow old and eventually die. Our passions die with us, but (fortunately or unfortunately) they never seem to grow old. Perhaps that's why Augustine wanted to spend his last days in vigorous prayer. He was seventy-six years old and weak, but he knew that he still had some time left for silliness, and he had a healthy fear that in his last moments he would demonstrate the truth of the saying: "There is no fool like an old fool."

## *Nostalgia for The Future*    15

Sometimes when we get older we mourn the loss of our past, saying:

> Oh, if I could only experience again the innocent days of my childhood, if I could only experience again the passionate love given and received in my youth, if I could only experience again the feeling of accomplishment and success of my mid-years! But now that I am old those days are lost forever, I can no longer look at life with simple wonder, believing that the unknown before me will be just fine. I can no longer look forward to being the "the end all and be all" of someone else's love, nor can I dare to give my love in such a passionate way. I can no longer speak to the world from the mountain of my accomplishment and success. No one is interested in what I say as I slide down the evening side of my life towards the grave.

So we sometimes moan, once we have come to age.
    When he was in his middle fifties, Augustine answered such sad nostalgia:

> You find humans who complain about their own times and say that the days of their parents were the really good times. But if they were able to go back to those old days they would complain about them too. You think that the good old days were good only because they are not *your* days now and therefore *must* be good. Why do you think the past was any

better than the present? From the Adam of yesterday to the Adam of today, the days are days of work and of sweat and thorns and trouble (S 346C, 1).

Despite the obvious fact that he could not have been having a very good day when he penned that sermon, Augustine's words contain the crucial truth that no age is an unmixed blessing. Those who are overcome with nostalgia for their youth don't seem to remember how it *really* was to be a kid.

For example, when I start complaining about how "fixed" my life is now that I am in my seventh decade, I should try to remember how frightened I was as I a child to have anything "unfixed." Now most of my life is memory, but then it seemed to be all possibility. And I did not like it a bit. Tiny apollonian that I was, I relished the structure of school and home. I liked the idea of knowing *exactly* what I would be doing day by day until my high school graduation. Beyond that I saw a vacuum, which I handled by a studied program of "not thinking." Too young to be drafted, my only insecurity during World War II was whether Dad would lose his job and be unable to provide me with the munificent ten-cent allowance that gave me access to the Saturday matinee movie mayhem that was the center of my social life.

Indeed, if we thought about it seriously, we would come to see that the good old days were not as glorious as we sometimes paint them to be. They sometimes seem so because we magnify the good things we remember—making the colors more brilliant, the tastes more pungent, the loves more ecstatic, and the victories more conclusive. In fact, the past was probably as grey and bland and unexciting as the present sometimes seems to be.

This came home to me one summer when I went back to the seashore where I had grown up. I was surprised to see how narrow the Boardwalk had become. In my memory it seemed just huge—in truth, larger than life. Of course, my first experience of that place was as a (relatively) small child. My revisiting was done as a lumbering adult. But there was something deeper in the difference.

When I make my past again present to me, it *always* seems smaller and shorter than it was in my memory. It must be that my imagination has taken the picture retained by memory and painted it with a larger brush, making it more expansive and color-filled than it actually was.

Perhaps we humans indulge such fantasy in order to cover over our worry about the possible narrowing and dimming of our future. As we look ahead to the setting sun and compare its dusk to the rosy dawn and brilliant noon of our lives, we console ourselves by saying: "Well, taken as a whole, my life has been mostly bright and cheery even though the present moment may be a bit dim."

It is an innocent fiction as long as it does not sour us on the good things left in our present. Indeed, it can even help us face our coming to age. Remembering a gently retouched past we may be able to hope for a more brilliant future—to hope that the "good old days" are yet to come.

## *Images of Life: Butterfly Wings*   16

One autumn day I walked through an ancient battle-field where men had lived and died for a cause that at the time seemed noble. The land was quiet now. Nature had covered over the bloody residue of human violence. Once a place of living death, on this day it had become a place of dying life as nature prepared itself for the winter darkness ahead.

As I walked along my autumn road I was suddenly surrounded by a flock of tiny butterflies, diminutive cousins of that great gold-and-black monarch breed that had sometimes shared my walks along the rocky New Hampshire coast. My present companions were only one-third the size of their Yankee relatives (barely an inch across with wings extended), but they shared the same rich coloring.

My little friends seemed happy as they fluttered along on fragile butterfly wings, enjoying immensely their day in the sun. I was not surprised at their joy. I knew something of their history. Most of their life had been spent blindly in the darkness of a nurturing cocoon or, as caterpillars, plodding painfully across the earth with their nose buried in the dirt, seeing nothing but what was immediately present to their narrow vision.

No wonder that they seemed so happy now. Now they were finally flying high, for only a day to be sure, but now they were at last flying high! Now they could see the beauty of the world that had been hidden from them in their pedestrian days. Now they could smell the flowers and drink their sweet nectar. Now they finally had a truly important task to perform: to fly from flower to flower, planting the seeds for a new spring that they could not even imagine, the spring that lay waiting just the other side of winter's darkness.

As I walked along surrounded by fluttering butterfly wings, it struck me that human life is not unlike theirs. We humans also spend much of our lives living in this world without being aware of its magic. At first we don't really do much except grow, getting ready for a mostly unknown future. When we finally break free and "go it alone" (as we say), we find that most of our days are spent in pedestrian tasks and simple thoughts. We don't have great dreams nor do we attempt noble tasks. Like caterpillars, we are pleased in just being able to conquer that stray pebble that blocks our way. We call any day a success if we have survived it, avoiding the disaster of being crushed by the rushing giants who cross our paths. We may carry in our being the very same colors that will mark our glory days, but we are too involved in just *existing* to see the beauty that is ours.

If we *do* survive, we too may enjoy a butterfly day—a time for flying high and wide, looking down at the earth and laughing in joy at how wonderful existence is. We may discover loves that we were never able to see before (so obsessed were we with ourselves) and spend happy hours fluttering along with them, just enjoying the warmth of the sun and the smell of the land. We may come to realize that we too have a noble purpose, the task of taking the sweetness of life and spreading it to others and thus preparing the world for the grand Spring that hides just beyond this life's Winter.

Indeed, we humans are very much like our butterfly friends. We too can have a day in the sun when we come finally to see the true meaning of ourselves and the world in which we live. We can come to see that we and the world reflect each in a special way the glory of God.

Like them, our day in the sun is not forever. In this life Winter comes for all of us and the time for flying is past. We humans die, but unlike the butterfly we can also grow old. Some of us are destined to live long after our days of glorious flight. But perhaps that is not a bad thing. The added time gives an opportunity to remember all our days, the dull as well as the brilliant. It gives us time to whet our appetite for that everlasting Spring that is just ahead.

I don't know what happens to butterflies when their evening comes. I can't remember seeing one dead nor one that looked particularly old. Who knows? Perhaps they explode into eternal spring while they are yet in the prime of life. Perhaps they do not even momentarily return to the darkness and dullness that marked their youth. Perhaps, as dusk deepens for them, God reaches down and snatches them into his world—the world that has no evening.

Perhaps that is what will happen to us humans too. After a short twilight we will be snatched from this earth to enjoy an eternal day with the Son who never sets.

It is a comforting thought now that the growing dusk announces the end of my day of flying high.

# *Sylvan Reflections of an Old Plant*  17

*(on the occasion of a lovely Rose's sixtieth birthday)*

Now that I have come of age, I see that we humans have much in common with our companions, the plants. Like them, we live through our seasons and the desire to have many springs is strong in us. We want to *live* long before we start looking around for someone to talk to. We are vegetables long before we adopt the pretense of being intellectual. In our baby years (and perhaps throughout life) we survive only because of the kindness of loves who feed us, and prune us, and water (or un-water) us as necessity demands. As tiny babies we were pleasant plants. We did not become *animals* till we hit the "terrible twos."

Even now in these our later years (when we claim to have our humble parts firmly in the control of spirit), our botanic roots come back to haunt us. In my experience even philosophers are affected. They seem to pursue "being" better after a plate of beans and a brew.

Now that my hair has silvered, I see that I am sylvan. Now in my seventh decade I have come to realize my true station in life—my *plant*-ation, if you will. Now I know that the story of any human life is like the rise and fall of a potted plant. When I was young I was all sleek and shiny (and also quite green and sappy). Now that I am old, my colors are more muted. I am somewhat mossy and must bear a pot out of proportion. Some would say that I have gone to seed, but that is only because they cannot see the passions of life still within my gnarled limbs and scarred trunk. They cannot see that I am still happy with my life, despite its many autumns and diminishing springs. Though covered with hoary leaves, I can still taste the sweetness of good water and feel the warmth of bright suns and be moved by the gentle breath of those who love me.

Living sixty or more years should not mean that an old plant (especially a lovely Rose like you) loses value. There is, after all, a Century Plant that is deemed quite extraordinary. If society so cherishes this Century Plant (*Agave Americana*), why should it look down on plants like you and me (*Americanus decrepitus*) who are just beginning to nibble their seventh decade? Indeed, our six decades of life till now are at least *real*. The supposedly "great" Century Plant lives much less than a hundred years. In fact, it lies around for ten years or so producing only spiky leaves. Then it flowers once and dies (probably from the effort), leaving behind orphan sprouts ignorant of their true mother or father.

It seems to me that the only valid justification for giving such a noble name to such a boring life is that when you must deal with someone who is all spiky leaves and no flowers, it just *seems* that they have been around for a hundred years. However, to be fair to *Agave Americana*, it should be noted that the flower it *does* produce in its one and only blossoming is quite huge, but that seems like an untoward explosion of color after so many grey years. The only lasting effects of all that blooming preparation and effort are offspring who are as dull and plodding as their parents.

How much better to be a lively Rose of sixty than a Century Plant waiting long years for something to happen! It is my experience that a Rose gets better with age. The fragrance deepens and broadens until it fills the entire world. For sure the delicate hues of budding youth are gone, but they are replaced with the deep reds and purples of a life warmed by many suns and enriched by many loves.

Who ever heard of a hummingbird going to a Century Plant for nectar? But a Rose mellowed with a taste of life is a source of sweetness to all who come to her. Moreover, a mature Rose can generate young who can really *know* her and together brighten the home where they live. These young sprouts bring joy by giving memories of *her* youth and by giving promise that the stream of life passing through her will last long into the future.

Moreover, when you are a human Rose, you know that sixty years is only the beginning of the beginning. It is no time at all for a flower destined to bloom forever. Being sixty is not a time for packing one's bags and waiting around morosely for the end of everything. Rather it is a time for remembering the past with fondness and celebrating the present that the past created and, indeed, for looking forward to a future without end—a future in a garden where the earth is always moist, and the sun is always bright, and the garden is filled with all those who touched and were touched in life by the fragrance of a lovely life.

You may be sixty now, my dear Rose, but that makes no difference to this old plant.

You will always be my very best frond.

## Graceful Aging                    18

**A**ll of us would like to die with dignity, but before that happens we would like to grow old with dignity.

In the Morning Prayer for Saturday (week 4), there is the following consoling promise from the Old Testament:

> The just will flourish like the palm-tree
>   and grow like a Lebanon cedar.
> Planted in the house of the Lord,
>   they will flourish in the courts of our God,
> still bearing fruit when they are old,
>   still full of sap, still green,
> to proclaim that the Lord is just.
>                     Ps 92:13-16

It is a dream of all of us to be like that in our waning years:

- still bearing fruit when we are old,
- still green and flourishing despite our somewhat gnarled limbs,
- still filled with life's juices,
- still filled with the great sap of life rather than *being* the great sap of life.

We don't want to end up as an oddity long past its prime, described by others as being out of contact with life "lo these many years."

We are scared when we see it happening to others. We are saddened when it happens to someone we love. Despite their past virtues and kindness, we are tempted to almost "hate" them in their querulous last years. And, when they die, we are sometimes left with a bad taste in our hearts, even though we don't like to admit it, even to ourselves. We suffer with them through their last years, sigh with relief when they depart, and then begin worrying that we will end up in the same condition, incapable of performing any useful function beyond causing other's blood to boil.

It does not need to be. Augustine's dictum that "we make our times" (S 80, 8) is as true for old age as for any other. There *is* no terminal disease of "nastiness" just waiting to infect us as we cross the line into our autumn or winter years. I remember speaking to a very senior confrere about how sad it was to see another member of the community become so obnoxious in his old age. It seemed that the promise of Psalm 92 had not worked for him. He, like us, had been "planted in the house of the Lord" (we were all members of a religious community) but that did not seem to prevent him from being terribly obstreperous and sappy in his last days. However, my other friend (who was indeed *much* older but who had managed to preserve the simplicity and optimism of youth with the wisdom of his many years) gave me a simple explanation: "What the heck (he said), the man did not get obnoxious when he got old. He always *was* obnoxious."

The point is interesting and is suggested by something that the old Augustine said long ago: "As we grow, we do not lose what we were before; we build on it." It is too late (apart from a great miracle) to be truly "planted in Christ" a few days before death. Rather we must grow up in Christ so that from our youth we may grow to be a perfect human being. If this happens then our infancy will be characterized by innocence, our childhood by reverence, our youth by virtue, our maturity by merit, and our old age by wise understanding (S 216, 7-8).

We need not worry about being graceful in old age if we were graceful as a child and as an adolescent and as a youth and in our middle age. We will continue to grow as we have been. If we are sap when we are young, we will be sap when we get old. The only difference in the periods will be the more numerous naps of our last years. But this "nappiness" will serve only to increase the intensity of our "sappiness," concentrating it in shorter periods of time.

And so, now that I have come of age, I should stop worrying about how I will be a year from now and begin trying to be as pleasant as I can be today. I must examine my roots today to see if they are planted in the garden of the Lord. If they are, then the slow movement I feel inside me is not my life's sappiness coming to the surface. Rather, it is the grace of the Lord preparing me for the eternal life that lies ahead.


*Paying for The Past*      **19**


Now that I have come to age, I spend as much time at my skin doctor as others spend at their dentists. Each time

I go he pops out a bit of skin that is either cancerous or precancerous. He tells me that I am now paying for my genes and my sins.

It seems that when I was younger I spent too many hours exposed to the summer sun:

- pursuing a short-lived career as a near-sighted first baseman on the sands of the Jersey shore,
- walking on the winter beaches of Florida,
- running with friends on the quiet beaches of Maine,
- sitting by the rocky shore of New Hampshire.

Now I am paying for such past exposure with recurring spots of skin cancer. It seems that we Irish stand shadow better than sun. At the time I felt just fine (as one always feels in the *midst* of frivolous debauchery), but now twenty years later I am paying for my solar sins.

It is not a terrible existence. When you get older you learn how to live with past excesses—overexposure to brilliance, nurturing ambitions that (in hindsight) were clearly foolish, dreaming of love that could never be realized. You can live with your scars as long as they do not point to a terrible hurt you brought to someone else. If you were the only one who lost pieces of skin or pieces of heart, you can look at the old wounds and say: "You old fool! Why didn't you have more sense?" But then you smile and remember that those "wild times"—lying too long in the hot summer sun, running too long after an impossible career, or pining too long for love that could never be yours—were part of the joy of being young and believing that you were indestructible and could never be hurt and could do anything you set your mind to and could win over anyone whom your heart desired.

When we come to age we learn the lesson that not all things are possible and that if we spend too much time lying on summer beaches or pursuing crazy dreams or dreaming about impossible loves, we will someday "pay the piper."

Our lives will be scarred by a brilliance that is simply too much to bear. Gaps in our being will be left by the absence of goals we dreamed about accomplishing and loves that we hoped would be ours exclusively and forever but were simply not meant to be. We go humbly to our healer to hear the diagnosis: "You must take better care. When you go out into the world use sun-screen and dream-block and take some potion that will stop you from loving too unrealistically." We take the advice to heart and follow it exactly (we old folks tend to obey our doctors better than we previously obeyed our elders) and live out the rest of our days in a more careful way.

It is frankly a somewhat boring existence, but we do have our memories. Now in the evening of our life, when we tend to our scars, or when we hear an old favorite song that we shared with someone long ago, we remember our days in the sun and smile. Truly we have been scarred by our past behavior, but such innocent profligacy has created for us grand memories, memories of life lived in the midst of brilliant summer days, a life that seemed to be *filled* with love and infinite possibilities.

As we now put healing lotions on the scars of our past, we remember how it felt to be truly *alive*. And through faith and hope we look forward to that future land of God where our greatest ambitions will be fulfilled—that land of cool beaches filled with love's laughter, that land where the air is always fresh and the sun never burns.

## *Old Learning*                    20

This life ends but learning goes on forever if we let it. When Augustine was in his sixtieth year, he wrote to St. Jerome asking for some information. He remarked that: "No age is too advanced to learn what needs learning because, although it is more fitting for old men to teach than to learn, it is even more fitting to learn what they teach than to remain ignorant" (E 166, 1).

Somewhat later on he refers to the Pharisee (John 3:10) who came at night to be taught, and he suggests that the reason for his coming in the dark was because he was ashamed by his need to learn. "For my part," Augustine continues, "it gives me greater pleasure to listen to a master than to be listened to as a master" (Ibid., 9).

That old age is a time meant for learning is an interesting idea. More often we concentrate on the "forgetting" part of being old, or we say that after a life of experience there is nothing new to be learned, nothing new to be seen. I find myself that now after years and years of traveling, I have little thirst for seeing new places. Every place seems much the same as any other when seen through my somewhat near-sighted, jaded vision.

But it is possible for the old to see familiar places in a new light when they see them through the eyes of someone else. It must be neat, for example, to be a grandparent of the very young. It gives you an excuse for doing with them many things that you would be embarrassed to do by yourself—like go to the zoo, or visit Disney Land, or play "catch" on the beach, or go down the water-slide at Ocean City. Though you have seen the whiteness of snow or the immensity of the sea a thousand times, you see it in a new way when you see it through the eyes of a little friend who is seeing it for the first time.

Long ago Augustine spoke about this wonderful fact. In a work on teaching the young, he wrote:

> Is it not a common experience that when we are showing certain lovely scenes about town or in the country to those who have never seen them, their pleasure in the new experience makes us see the scene with a new delight . . . even though we passed it day after day without seeing it because

it was too "usual" for us? This new appreciation becomes deeper in direct proportion to the intensity of our affection for them. One with them in the bond of love, the old is made new for us through their joy (DCR, 12.17).

The nice thing about showing youngsters the world for the first time and learning from them again the wonder of the world, is that any eccentricity is allowed to the old when you are with a little one. When "ancients" run on the beach by themselves, onlookers search for their CPR manual. When they run with a child, others smile at the gracious scene and pull out their cameras. It makes us "old fogies" act differently too. On our own, we tend to "strut" through amusement parks as though we were on important business. If we dare to ride the merry-go-round, we do so with serious faces—as though we were state safety inspectors forced to ride on the "horsey" for the sake of the young. But if we do the same ride with a two-year old, we feel free to share their fun. We imitate their innocent humility without embarrassment—even trying for the "golden ring" to please *them* (of course it is *not* that we would *ever* want it for ourselves).

With the very young we can experience again the joy of the toy store. Without them, we visit hardware stores—those sublimated toy stores for ancient bachelors.

With or without young companions, we must continue to learn when we have come to age. The beginning of such learning is to realize that there is still much to know. As Augustine wrote to a friend: "If we don't understand that we don't understand, we are in danger of understanding nothing at all" (E 159, 2). Without such humble awareness, all future learning is impossible. The humility of children is wise if they strive to overcome their ignorance. The wisdom of the old is humble if they realize that with all their experience they have just begun to know and that the opportunity for learning never ends—in time or in eternity.

The aging Augustine gave very good advice indeed when

he told his friends: "Let your old age be childlike and your childhood like old age. You must do this lest your wisdom be filled with pride and your humility be without wisdom" (ENN 112, 2).

The new is not behind us. It is ahead of us no matter how old we are. We must be careful not to let "oldness" take over our lives. We must grow and make progress. Our bodies may be falling apart, but our spirit can be renewed day by day. "Let's not age in a way that makes us become old. Let newness grow in us" (ENN 131, 1).

## *Images of Life: The Sower*                   21

**W**hen Augustine was at the midpoint of his life, he wrote: "As one scatters grain which he had carefully gathered, so we must pour out our life in order to find it forever" (S 313D).

This vision of human life as a sower sowing seeds was to remain a favorite image for him throughout his long life, one that he put into practice till the very end. He faced his death with good cheer and continued to give himself to the needs of others. He was convinced that as soon as he began to withdraw his life from others, as soon as he began to "save" himself, locking up his gifts in the silent silo of his "self," his life would rot and for all intents and purposes he would perish. He believed firmly in the human truth repeated in Scripture: "A person must lose life in order to save it" (Cf. Matt 16:25).

To sow one's life freely to the world is often easier said than done. When we were young, we were exorbitant with our lives, pursuing the venture of the moment with no thought of saving ourselves for tomorrow. We "threw ourselves" into each day in the absolute confidence that we were not losing anything of importance. So what if this particular passion was unproductive! Our seed was unlimited and if this particular batch was "wasted," there was still plenty left for the next adventure. Others smiled and said we were "sowing our wild oats" and agreed with us that the day would come when our lives would settle down, our fields would become quiet, and the first green shoots of an important life would appear on the earth.

When we grow older we tend to think that our days for sowing life are over, that we must preserve the precious energy left to us for the harvest. We no longer seek new challenges. We spend our time "taking naps" so that we can have the energy for the next day, a day which will be spent in "taking naps" for the day following. We say that "my life is over, and now I must rest," and in the resting we fulfill our assertion.

Of course, there is little we can do about the gradual lessening of our physical powers, but "sowing one's life" is not a physical exercise. It is an exercise of the spirit by which we remain open and interested in the world around us and the time before us. We may no longer be able to make persuasive speeches that will cure the troubled, but we can listen sympathetically to those who need a "listener." We can continue to love others by allowing them to love us, perhaps allowing them to "take care of us" and thus sow their own seed of good works in the world. At very least we can try to avoid being obstreperous, showing how one can live a life of faith and hope and kindness even into old age. Sometimes we sow our best seeds by not being a weed in someone else's garden.

Even in our death the image of the sower endures, but now it is an image of what death is really like. A burial is not a particularly pleasant event for those who must stand by the side of the grave. It seems so *final*. The loved one is gone. We shall never again enjoy the fruit of their physical presence. They exist for us now only in our memory. They are buried in the earth and that is that! But Augustine suggests that people of faith who know what is truly happening get a quite different picture. They see us burying our love and say: "Do not be sad. That which is buried in the furrows of this earth is no longer in the granary nor in your hands, but someday you shall return to this field and be overwhelmed and delighted to see beauty where now you weep for the barrenness of the opened earth" (S 361, 9).

Through the years of human history, we harvest again and again the fruit from the lives of our dear ones who have sowed their love in our hearts. But this harvest will be nothing compared to harvest of humanity itself that will take place at the end of time. Then the earth will open, and truly we shall begin to enjoy the fruit of our labors. Having thrown our lives away in time, we shall gain them for all eternity. Having lost our loves for a time, we shall enjoy them everlastingly in that deathless land where finally and forever we shall be at home with our flesh and blood.

## *Marion's Work*     22

Augustine once wrote: *Pondus meum, amor meus; eo feror, quocumque feror* ("My love is my weight, drawing me wheresoever I am drawn") (C 13.9). He could just as well have said *Pondus meum, labor meus* ("My *work* is my weight, moving me into my future"). Most of us have a compelling need to have something worthwhile to do. We seem to need some fine work to pull us outside ourselves. We feel such need perhaps because we are afraid that if we remain too long inside ourselves, we will find that we are nothing much at all.

It is not a good fact nor does it even make good sense, but it is a fact none the less, that most of us need to be "doing something" to have a sense of self-worth. Meeting a stranger on a plane, we seldom ask "Who are you?" Rather, we ask "What do you do?" and in light of their answer we determine whether or not they are worthy of further interest.

To be old and lose your job or to be old and be unable to get a job (though you *know* you can do the job) is a traumatic experience. You come to believe that the only reason for your rejection is that you are old and "oldness" is taken as *prima facie* evidence that you can no longer *do* anything worthwhile—and, as an implicit corollary, that you no longer *are* anything worthwhile.

It may be even harder to bear (if you have made your work your life), to *have* a job and slowly become aware that you cannot "cut it" anymore, that you are stale, just going through the motions, losing the verve that made you good at what you spent your life doing. When you are fired you can at least get justifiably mad at somebody else, but who do you get mad at when you lose your fire?

Coming to age means for many of us a change of occupation, either facing a future of no work or a future of new work. Coming to age sensibly means that we must face this prospect and deal with it. We cannot fight the inevitable. It is as silly to refuse "to grow old" as it is to refuse "to grow up." It is true that our spirit never ages, but it can grow in wisdom and part of being wise is to make accommodations to that other part of our being that *does* grow up, grow old, and wear down. When we begin to burn out or wear down, we should heed Augustine's advice to "bend to it lest you be broken" (DCR, 15.20).

Such bending can be helped by the conviction that there is another work for us to do, a work that is indeed more important than anything else we have tried to do. Even when he was in his middle forties and still very actively involved in the world around him, Augustine could yet realize that his great life work was himself—making of himself a decent human being and a worthy child of God. He also recognized that it was a "difficult field to work, a place of too much sweat" (C, 10.16).

What we do with ourselves at any age has an impact on the world, and this is true even when we reach a state where we cannot do much else. My friend Marion is a proof of that. I buried Marion a few years back at age seventy-five. She was an artist and in her last years she concentrated on pictures of Christ at various stages of his life. Her last picture was a head of Christ as he might have looked standing before Pilate, just after he heard the fateful words: "Nothing more can be done."

Those words meant a lot to Marion because twelve years before she had heard the same words from her doctors. She had a back operation that did not work, and when she asked the doctors if at least they could do something to relieve the pain, they responded: "We are sorry, Marion. Nothing more can be done."

And so she lived the last twelve years of her life in pain. Despite her disability she continued her painting, mostly from her bed. After two years of work, the head of Christ was almost completed, except for the eyes. Marion could not seem to get the eyes just right. And so one day she struggled into the bathroom, put the picture on the sink, and painted her *own* eyes into the face of Jesus Christ. The result is striking. As you stand before the picture and look at the swarthy, suffering face of Christ, you can see looking back at you the sky-blue eyes of Marion.

The picture is a symbol of Marion's life in her last years. She infrequently could leave her little Welfare-subsidized apartment, so the world came to her. Children, the very old, the sick, the upset would come to visit—not to make Marion feel better, but so *they* could feel better. Somehow or other, coming into her presence, one could feel the presence of God; one could feel that the eyes of Jesus Christ were looking back at you from the face of Marion.

Marion had to give up her active life because of her disability, but in so doing she found her work. She would be first to admit that she was not a saint, but that just goes to prove that we need not be perfect to be a place where God can work. God wants us only to be as good as we can be, and that may be far from saintly perfection.

Anyone of us can participate in the great work of making the Divine present to our world. Old or young, we are all places of God, but when we are old we sometimes get a greater opportunity to make that place better. When we achieve great age, others tend to stop asking us to do inconsequential things, and we then can come to realize that there is no better work for us to do than to make Christ so real in us that others can see his shining eyes smiling at them from our somewhat wrinkled faces.

## *The Rescuers and The Rescued* 23

Augustine wrote that we prove our love to a loved one when we bear the other's burden (DDQ, 71.1). It is also a therapeutic exercise. When all is going well and we are swinging through life with all those we love seemingly doing just fine, we may tend to concentrate all our attention upon ourselves, saying: "Am *I* happy?" "Am *I* fulfilled?" "Am *I* loved?" "Am *I* treated with proper respect?"

All this changes when someone we love with a deep and a true love falls ill or suffers some disaster. Their need forces us out of ourselves. We empty ourselves of ourselves, leaving more room for them and for God. We pray to God to come to our love with healing and to come to us with wisdom and courage so that we will know what to do and have the strength to do it day in and day out as long as need be. We devote our energies to "rescuing" our love, and in bearing their burden we forget about ourselves.

But such "rescuing" cannot go on forever. Sometimes we will need others to bear *our* burdens. Augustine makes this point through an analogy of a herd of deer crossing a dangerous channel:

> When deer must swim across a swirling stream to an island in order to find a new pasture, they organize themselves in a single line so that, as they swim, the heavy weight of their antlered head can be supported by the flank of the deer ahead. The buck at the front has no support but after a time he will yield his place to the second in line and himself go to the rear where he too may take some rest. In this way the entire group of deer, by bearing one another's burden, are able to cross even the most difficult channel to solid ground (DDQ, 71.1).

The plan seems ideal, but in fact in human life it does not always work out that way. Some humans yield the front of the line reluctantly, while others seem to spend their entire life looking for a willing haunch on which to rest their weary head. Some individuals seem to make a profession of being rescuers. Others make a profession of being objects of rescue. Some, of course, have no choice. Their weakness comes from a disability truly beyond their control. Others, however, have taken the role of "suffering soul" voluntarily. These are adult children who refuse to take responsibility for their lives. They are constantly beating a path to others for comfort, solace, and support.

Those being "rescued" constantly and who in fact have no permanent disability (beyond their inability to cope with life) must realize that "being rescued" in not a way of life for the relatively healthy human. It is meant to be only a sometime necessary event in the lives of most. Hence, they must look forward to the day and strain forward to the day when they can have the strength to take their turn at the head of the line—if not supporting others, and least not demanding that others support them when it is not truly necessary.

The rescuers on the other hand must not believe that they are strong enough to stay at the head of the herd forever. Even the strongest buck or doe needs some rest. They are limited in their powers to bear other's burdens and if they do not humbly admit that fact, they are likely to become broken by the constant demands on their good nature.

Those who have spent their lives being rescuers must be prepared to face the coming to age that will force upon them the role of one in need of rescue. Allowing others to bear one's burden is as important as bearing the burdens of others. Refusing to accept one's true need is a sign that something is missing in life—that healthy humility which guarantees safe passage to a land of good pastures, a healthy humility that is willing to accept present fragility even after a lifetime of supporting others.

## *Circles Outside Circles*   24

When I was very young the good Sisters of St. Joseph exerted great effort in making of me a legible (if not great) writer. In those days the famous Palmer method was in vogue, and young ruffians all over the nation spent long afternoons filling copybooks with smooth spirals which were supposed to glide effortlessly across page after page—circles begetting circles endlessly into infinity.

I am not sure what effect this had on my writing (though I become an artist when any sentence has many "Os"), but now I see that the exercise had much deeper meaning. During all those long afternoons as I spiraled away my time, I was drawing pictures of my life—a life of meshing and separating circles—a life that rolls along touching, embracing, and then separating from the circles of lives of others.

Now that I have come of age, I can look back and see those precious moments when I rolled along my path entwined with caring loves and important projects. Now that I have come of age, I can see that more and more I am falling out of such accustomed circles. The spirals on my last page will stand outside the circles of earthly loves and earthly projects. Just as I entered time alone, I shall enter eternity alone. The last mark that I shall make in my copybook will be a solitary spiral that spins off the page into eternity.

The separations that come with getting older are facts that must be faced and accepted if we are to write our last page with equanimity and good cheer. But it is a hard thing to do: to find oneself falling outside the circle of other lives.

Now that I have come of age, I perceive that more and more it is happening to me: I am falling out of the accustomed circles of my life. Friends who once were deep and true have moved on, swept perhaps by the currents of their lives into new circles which have no place for me. There is nothing angry about our separation. It is no one's fault particularly. It is just that now we must do our spirals in different books. Children grow up; friends move on to new lives and new interests; old companions fill their books and end their time. Those who are living, if reminded of us, will say: "Oh yes! I knew him well and care for him still. By the way . . . what is he doing now?" Past loves are remembered with fondness, but if perchance we meet them again there is no longer a passionate embrace—only a polite passing grappling. We kiss the air beside the face whose lips we once warmly touched.

This separation of circles happens too in careers. Once a mover and shaker in one's work, you wake up one day to find that you have fallen outside the circle of power. Once others came to you when something was needed to be done or when prudent advice was required. Now they come with hints about the advantages of early retirement. After so many years of complaining about the burden of responsibility and proclaiming your passionate desire for peace, you find one day people indeed leaving you alone. They stand in the corner whispering about the great problems and plans they have for the institution, leaving you to finish a leisurely lunch. The grand project rolls on, but you sit on the side of the road reminiscing *ad nauseam* about the "good old days" to any unfortunate soul you can entrap. You say you have *chosen* not to apply for new prestigious jobs, but inside you are a little hurt that no one pressures you to change your mind. You get excited when you are approached to be on a committee searching for vibrant, young replacements for those soon to retire—until you realize that you are one of the "old fogeys" they intend to replace.

When you were younger this "falling out of old circles of love or power" was easier to bear because you yourself were rolling along "merrily, merrily" in pursuit of life's dream. Passing loves and jobs were not missed. Some of them you caused to be missed yourself and as for the others, you may have been sad for a day, but your present was too full and your future too promising for past regrets to linger long.

Now that you are older the "falling out" can be harder to accept because you realize that you are no longer "leaving others in your wake." Your separation comes from your stillness, not your activity. You have slowed up and your loves and the world itself have rushed ahead, leaving you behind. Sometimes your situation can be made bearable if you have a few old friends left who share your measured pace, and it can be even enjoyable if you have an old love who is joined to you in your slowing circle. But sometimes even these supports are taken away (old friends and old loves may die before us), and we must face the task of finishing the spiraling exercise of our life alone—still physically with this world and its people, but truly on the outside looking in.

I, like every person who comes to age, must prepare for this stillness that comes with separation from accustomed circles. I must try to see that my slowing up, my separations from the fast-moving world around me, are caused by my beginning the last and most grand circle of life— that one which will eventually spin me beyond time. I move at more measured pace now because I am moving in a larger circle. I am approaching the limits of all time on that outermost circle of life.

Down below I can see others spinning and whirling like firecrackers in tight sparkling circles, rushing this way and that between places and projects and people. I am far removed from all that hustle and bustle. I move in stately solitary splendor carefully outlining in my somewhat ragged book that final great cycle of my life. I move slowly now, but only because I have all eternity to take my time.

## *Humble Tolerance*   25

Scripture seems to speak to me in different ways at different periods of my life. Thus, I have read the story of the woman taken in adultery (John 8) many times but it is only recently (now that I have come to age) that I begin to understand why the elderly were the first to leave when Christ said "Let the man among you who has no sin be the first to cast a stone at her" (John 8:7). When you are old you have more to remember.

One who has lived for a long time is likely to be less surprised by and more tolerant of the foibles of others. Looking at their past humbly, they either see that they have fallen into the same perversity themselves or were saved from it by the luck of the draw. The old folk in the gospel story were the first to leave probably because they suddenly remembered all of their past passions (and perhaps a few that were still present).

Their alacrity in leaving is encouraging. It shows that some of us in our later years can develop a humble tolerance of others. Living a long life can cause us to have greater sympathy and hope for others. Seven years out of his own pre-conversion days of misery, Augustine remarked that "similarity in misery softens the hardness of the human heart, however hard it may be" (S 259, 3). When you have had your own bouts with selfishness or passion or greed or confusion or stupidity, you can understand it better in others. You put up with those who are malicious or mixed up, remembering how you were tolerated by friends and family when you were in the same condition.

Of course, such toleration is always of the person, not of the evil they do. The memory of the hurt caused by your own past sins makes you intolerant of the *sins* of others, but the memory of your own condition in your sinning makes you understanding now of the *person* sinning. And furthermore, the memory of your surviving your past craziness, makes you hope that this *other crazy* will somehow survive, too, and gives you the patience to wait for the grace of God to have its way. You come to see the truth of Augustine's statement: "If you don't forget your own past, you will never despair of those who *are* now what you once *were*" (ENN 50, 24). You say with him: "We need not despair of any human being as long as they are alive" (ENN 36/2, 11).

Unfortunately, sometimes this humble tolerance does not come with age. Sometimes we become more vicious with age. With little to do, the elderly have more time on their hands to think about the real or imagined sins of others. It is sad when this happens. Old or young, all of us share the same condition. We are all in an inn, a place where pilgrims may heal and rest in preparation for the eternal life ahead. You would expect that we who have come to age would be more tolerant of our fellow "INN-mates." After all, we are likely to check out soon. You would think we would spend more time planning for the trip and less time bickering with others about which of us has the most noble defect.

Perhaps our problem is that we come to forget our past. Augustine suggests that the less we concentrate on our own sins, the more interested we become in the sins of others (S 19, 2-3). We focus on the mistakes of others when we come to think that we have never made a mistake, that we have never nor ever will need healing. This is just a sign that our moral illness has reached our mind. Our problem is not a physical passion but a pride-induced amnesia. We cannot see that Augustine's warning has any reference to us: "Who is always good? If God were to sift through your life, he could more easily find perversity in your present, than you could find virtue in your past" (S 47, 5.6).

Augustine was convinced that the first sign of our own healing is to be found in our kindness to others. He told his people: "My friends, in the midst of the present mixed-up condition of life, your own healing begins when you do not look down on any other human" (ENN 30/2, 7). His advice is valuable for every age, but it is especially valuable for the old. We may not be able to do much else at the end of our lives, but at least we can be kind. Kindness does not involve any heavy lifting, and it is not fattening. We need not extend ourselves or harm ourselves when we try to put up with others who now are as mixed up as we once were.

If we honestly recall what was or what could have been in our own past, it is unlikely that we will ever be the one to cast the first stone at another. In that humble tolerance we shall find our salvation.

*Images of Life: The Lamp* **26**

Augustine suggests that our lives just now are something like a burning lamp. Our hunger and thirst day after day are signs that the sources of our energy are constantly being expended and need to be replenished. We eat and drink for a few moments, and this is enough to last a day. We fill up our store quickly, and it is consumed bit by bit over a longer period of time. When we are almost empty, we feel the pangs of hunger or thirst, like the flickering light of a lamp, calling out for a renewal of its precious store of oil. Once replenished, our life continues to burn merrily away for another day.

A naïve child may believe that the life of the body, like the light of the lamp, is eternal. All you need do is pour in more oil. When you are young you can be convinced that your recuperative powers are eternal, that all you need do to live brightly forever is to refuel from time to time with a little food and a little drink and a little sleep. When you are young and feeling good every moment of every day, it is hard to see the truth in Augustine's words: "The body is indeed just like a lamp. Even if you put oil into it everyday, it cannot always burn. Sooner or later the wick itself will waste away and it, like us, will eventually be consumed by old age" (S 362, 11). It is interesting to me (now in my seventh decade) that Augustine wrote these words when he was fifty-six years old in the context of a sermon about the next life. At fifty the dissolution of one's wick becomes all too evident. At fifty you become more interested in resurrection than restoration.

Of course, as he will say in another place, we only grow old on the outside, "even though the timbers of your body are weighed down and creaking with years" (E 147, 2), but that is the part that hurts when I get up in the morning, that is the part that falls asleep just when I am on the verge of some important discovery, that is the part that comes up with a strange new pain that prophesies a shortened future.

My spirit may still be young, but that can increase my distress. I have not lost my youthful passions, just the power to exercise them. I have not lost my great ambitions, just the time to accomplish them. And I have not lost any of that youthful perceptiveness which makes it painfully clear that "my years come in order that they may go . . . and that as they pass through me they leave behind a person who is increasingly less strong" (S 109, 4). My ageless spirit makes me realize the fact that "just as my hair slowly grows day by day, so my earthly life slowly fades day by day" (ENN 38, 12), and "that my increasing feebleness is an extension of my future death into my present life" (ENN 84, 10).

The strength of my young spirit is not shown in ignoring my age, but in recognizing it. The continuing powers of my spirit are demonstrated not in vain attempts to overcome the deterioration of my "wick" but in accepting it and dealing with it. I am not dead yet. My light has not yet gone out and though it may flicker from time to time, it still can brighten the lives of those around me and maybe even enlighten a few. There *is* life after tennis. A movement from "rock and roll" to a rocker *does not* end life. I still have a bit of oil in my lamp and there are still people to love and interesting projects to accomplish. As long as I have a little flame left in me, there is no need to bring additional darkness to the lives of those who surround me.

If I fulfill Augustine's somber statement that "when a man grows old, he is full of complaints" (S 81, 8), it will be my own fault. And the fault will be precisely this: I did not accept the strengths of my weakened condition and did not make the best of the earthly life that was left to me.

## My Place                                     27

Now that I have come to age, I feel an increasing thirst for some private place where I can be "at home":

- a place where I can retreat and be myself,
- a place where I can be naked body and soul if I so desire,
- a place where others may not enter without my leave,
- a place where I can be free of pretending to "be" what others expect me to be,
- a place where I can be what I am, a child afraid of losing love, a man afraid of age and death.

My private place must be a place of space and light. I need to be able to stretch my body and mind, to a have a "here and there" so that I can walk to and fro in space and time. I don't want to be able to touch the walls that enclose my life. I don't want to feel the ceiling press down on me. I want a window to the outside of my life so that I can see others working out their destiny.

This need becomes especially strong when you get older. When you are young, you don't feel it so much. You are too distracted by a busy life. You have no true home. With all the coming and going, you end up being neither here nor there. Constantly on the move, you end up with two addresses, four phone numbers, and frustrated friends. They call and the message is always the same: "He is in some other place." After a while they give up, and despite all your addresses and phones, you find that no one contacts you. You end up having past acquaintances and no loves present to you. You have spent your life being "no place special."

Endured for a long time, this "being no place special" creates the conviction that you are "no one special." Others get tired of looking for you, and you yourself begin to forget who you are. Like the tip of a pendulum on a grandfather clock, you swing from place to place impelled by forces beyond your ken, and you gradually lose sight of the works that make you tick.

Sometimes when you are young, you cannot avoid the movement. Your work demands travel, but each new place is a place for work rather than a home. You have no time to set roots before you must move again. Your place is no more than a job-place, a place where you spend time working out a present assignment as you wait for the next. These new places are not necessarily unpleasant if they afford decent food and shelter and some quiet to think. But after a while (as you get older) you begin to dream of retirement and getting some permanent place where you can be at home.

It is a terrible thing to be "homeless" in this life or in the next—to be a wanderer in a land that was never meant for you. The central pain of hell is to know that you are not "at home" and never will be. The pain of the homeless in this life is to know that you have no home to go to, and others do not care.

The business traveler does not mind so much giving up one job-place after another as long as there is hope for something better. These job-places are never really yours. But to lose a *home*-place that is *yours*—that is indeed almost *you* since it contains so much of your history, so many dreams, so much memory of love experienced—to lose such a place can take away the desire to live.

It is hard for anyone to lose "their special place," but it can be especially traumatic for the old. One of the burdens of age is that sometimes such loss of one's home, one's private place, becomes necessary. Sometimes the burdens of a "big old house" become too much and the person is forced to move to an apartment—usually a place which is pleasant enough but without character, a place not for "being at home" but for waiting for the next major event in life: its ending.

This sense of "losing one's place" may be even more traumatic when one is forced to enter a nursing facility at the very end. There truly you have no place of your own. You may be "cared for" quite well, but it is hard to feel truly "at home." This is what happened to my mother. For the last two years of her life, her body lay trapped in someone else's place, but her mind was free to wander through any past memory or create any present fantasy. In those secret places of her mind, she created "her place"—a private place that could be entered by no one else but herself and her God.

Perhaps that is the only private place, the only "place of our own" that any of us have. It is the only place that is with us through all time and eternity. Augustine (who hated to travel) kept reminding himself and his people that there is no "lasting city" anywhere this side of death. Every house we dwell in here is at best an inn for travelers (ENN 34, 6). No place here can ever be a permanent home.

That being said, I would still like a room in this pilgrim's inn with a lock on the door and a private bath and a large window with a good view. Happy in an exterior place at least temporarily my own, I can then set about the task of decorating my "private place" within for the travels that lie ahead.

## *Living Inside Oneself* 28

Augustine was firmly convinced that the one place where humans can find peace in this life is deep inside themselves. He says: "It is there that you cry out, there you are heard, there you are made happy. . . . This is what the Lord means when he says (Matt 6:6): 'Go to your room, close your door and pray to our Father in private. Then your Father, who sees what no man sees, will repay you' " (ENN 33/2, 8). Himself a man busy about the world for most of his life, he would yet proclaim: "I find that it is impossible for me to taste and enjoy that which is really good without getting some relief from the care and toil of daily life. Believe me, a person has a great need to somehow withdraw from the turmoil of these things that are passing away if they are to be ever able to say: "I am not afraid" (E 10, 2).

Now that I have come to age, I can see the truth in what he says. The one refuge in time of trouble is within. If you are able to withdraw inside and be at peace with yourself, happiness is possible even under the worst of conditions. It is inside that you can find that cell of silence that no one else can touch. This quiet place is unaffected by what other people say about you, what events do to your "outside." In turmoil you can withdraw within and quietly put into perspective the events of the day.

Even the most peaceful world becomes a place of distress if this cell of self is disturbed. It is then that we fly to public places to be distracted by the noise of others. Augustine likens it to a husband and wife having trouble at home. He writes:

> Listen carefully, my friends. People with crabby spouses do not like to go home. They go instead to the city square and there find a little peace. When the time comes when they *must* go home, they become sad because they know what they will face: bickering, badgering and bitter confusion. When there is fighting at home, there can be no order and it seems better by far to leave and wander around outside for a while. Such spouses are truly in a sorry state, but worse by far are those who fear to enter into themselves because of the conflict in their own hearts (ENN 33/2, 8).

Sometimes we need external help to find our inner place of peace. It is hard to retreat inside when we are being forced outside by pain or illness or sorrows. How much easier it is when we have an external place where we can feel at home: a bench by the sea, a favorite chair in a bright airy room, the embrace of one who loves us. In such an external place of peace, it seems easy to turn our attention inside and there find ourselves.

There too we can find again our earthly loves. Though separated from them by space, time, or even death itself, we need only to go inside ourselves to meet them again—to walk in memory along deserted ocean beaches and quiet forest trails. Indeed, when I go inside I am never alone. Good friends come and visit and we relive the past. There I can recall a brief happy moment and make it forever. I can make my own world inside, and thereby cope with the world outside that I cannot control.

It is also there deep inside that I can find God. Augustine tells me that God is reflected in every part of creation, but that the most perfect image is found within my spirit. Thus if I "squander myself by throwing myself away . . . always living outside myself . . . I waste myself" (IJE 25, 15). Like the young, wandering Augustine, I cannot even find myself, much less God (C 5,2).

Now that I have come to age, I can understand the quiet that sometimes comes over the very old. They are not necessarily "losing contact with reality." They may indeed finally be getting in contact with reality—spending more and more time in that quiet bright place that their lived wisdom has built inside—that place where there is no age, where their spirits are ever young dancing before the God who is more ancient than time. This is the God who can make even the oldest of us young when we return to him deep inside our very selves (ENN 39, 4).

## Stillness                                    29

God is only heard in stillness, and to be truly still is almost impossible for you and me. We are swept along by the stream of time. Day in and day out we are on the move, tossed here and there by the currents of our lives, now reaching out for this security, now that—always failing because all that we grasp is moving as fast as we.

In the context of his meditation on time, Augustine describes the human condition very accurately (as he very well could since it was the story of his own life):

> Humans find it hard to taste the sweetness of eternity because they cannot still their thoughts rushing vainly back and forth between what has been and what is yet to come. . . . If only someone could make their hearts stay still for a little while, so that then for a moment they could be enraptured by the splendor of that eternity that is always still . . . Who indeed can grasp the hearts of humans so that they will stand still and see? . . . Can any words of mine accomplish such a grand task? (C, 11.11).

The answer to Augustine's last question is of course: "No!" There are no words that can still the human mind. But growing old can. Now that I have come to age, I perceive a natural stillness forced upon me. I am now out of the mainstream. I have spun off into a quiet pool of slowly revolving moments. I am not tempted to rush back into my past—mulling over "what might have been," proudly reliving (and enhancing) past triumphs. I no longer have the energy to dream of grand projects yet to be accomplished in the time left to me. I live now only in a quiet present.

Now that I have come of age, stillness seems close to me. The violent eruptions of my life are over and done with. My present moments are now more like warm lava slowly moving over the landscape, hiding the fire within. Stillness has been given to me. What shall I do with it? Will I spend my days digging deep inside myself to find that warm eternal light within? Or will I stand back and watch my life harden into immobility as I sit mesmerized by the fantasy and trivial games of T.V., spending my precious days of stillness in "not thinking at all"?

The deadness of mind which I used to blame on constant movement can be part of the stillness of my aging,

too, if I don't watch out. If it happens I will have no one
to blame but myself. I will have missed eternity by not us-
ing well the last time of my life.

## *Listening*　　　　　　　　30

With the quietness of age comes the opportunity for
listening. Indeed, sometimes listening is forced upon us. As
an old friend said one day: "After long years spent in ac-
quiring experience, I find now that no one is interested in
my wisdom. Once you retire from the mainstream of daily
activity, no one expects your views to make that much sense
any more." Once you come to age you find that the world
gives you a lot more time for listening.

The experience is not all bad. It can be a relief to sit back
and no longer be expected to make sensible statements. For
the first time in your life, you have the opportunity to analyze the absurdity of others, the time to appreciate the innocent wisdom of children, the chance to listen and hear
what friends are *not* saying—to perceive the deepest feelings quietly revealed by their inattention—like going to your
retirement party and suddenly finding yourself on the outside of a circle busily centered on someone else who speaks
to them of the future rather than the past.

Listening may be the last and best activity of a long life.
It is certainly the "in" thing to do these days in scientific
circles. All over the world astronomers are listening to the
heavens with sophisticated instruments. They search for
some evidence that we humans are not alone in the universe,
that there is some life, especially some rational life out there
beyond our day by day earthly experience. We hear of their
efforts and applaud, saying to ourselves: "Who knows? Perhaps if there is a thinking, caring person out there beyond
our earth, they may even think of *me* and care for *me.*"

My mentor St. Augustine would be much in favor of such investigations, I think. He sang of the wonders of the universe many times in his writings and preaching. Perhaps he would have wondered at the use of such an immense amount of money to listen to the words of an alien intelligence, when the cries of the poor on earth go unanswered. But in principle he would make no objection to listening quietly for the sounds of alien friends. He was much in favor of having friends, and he would not have been reluctant to investigate distant places to find new acquaintances that he could talk to and learn from and perhaps love.

What *would* amaze him would be the paradox of humans spending a lifetime listening to the heavens for some spark of intelligence while spending no time at all listening for some sign of a Lord of Heavens. He declared himself mystified by those in his own day who were experts at predicting future eclipses of the sun but could not see their own eclipse that was taking place before their eyes day after day. He puzzled over humans who are overcome by the wonders of their new knowledge of the stars but take for granted the wondrous power *inside* which allows them to understand the world *outside* (C, 5.3-4). He was convinced that listening is of little advantage to human life if it only deals with what is outside—if we listen to the galaxies and the sun and the moon and the planets, if we listen to crashing seas and whistling winds and the sounds of animals and the words of humans, but never listen to ourselves and what is happening inside ourselves.

When we are busy in the world it is easy to be trapped by what is outside us. Augustine himself spent a good portion of his life doing exactly that. He ran around the world looking for that Infinite One who would know him and care about him, but everywhere he went the world outside cried: "I am not the one you seek!" (C, 10.6). At last he turned away from the world out there and began to search the universe within himself.

He listened quietly for the God Within to speak, and he eventually came to hear him. He came to perceive that the strongest argument for his being touched by the Infinite, for the Infinite dwelling not simply *among* humans but *in* humans, was the fact that he was drawn to the Infinite. For reasons he could not explain he, a dying human, dreamed of living *forever*; he, a confused human, wanted to know *everything*; he, a self-centered human, sought a *perfect* love; he, a human who often acted like something less than he was, yet thirsted to be something more than he could be. He found in himself infinite dreams and infinite thirsts and infinite ambitions, and he finally saw that these must have their source in some Infinity beyond his ken.

It was then that he began to appreciate the quiet times of his life and to sit back and listen to the movement of the Infinite deep inside his own being. It was then that he heard the first whisper of that alien voice from a distant place—the voice of that being who had come a far distance to be *in* him because (for some inexplicable reason) he *loved* him.

By careful listening Augustine was able to hear that Infinite that wanted to be his friend forever, that Infinite that was even now part of his present. By careful listening the old Augustine was able to hear wisdom. By careful listening the old Augustine found Infinite Love.

And so too may it happen for me, now that I have come to age and have been given time to listen to the sounds of eternity.

## *Images of Life: Grasping at Twigs*   31

One of Augustine's favorite images for human history and for each individual's life is that of a river rushing towards a distant Great Falls. He writes:

> As a torrent is formed from the rains and eventually breaks through its narrow banks and runs roaring down the slopes until it finally finishes its course, so it is with each of our lives. Indeed, the whole human race, gathered together from hidden sources, rushes through time until it dies, falling again into a hidden place. Thus, this passing state that we call our life roars and rushes away (ENN 109, 20).

We are rushing into our future towards the Falls and if we paid attention, we could hear the crashing of the falling waters even now. We are not especially happy about the prospect. We spend much of our energy trying to stay where we are, grasping at twigs to pull ourselves ashore into some quiet eddy where we can rest and "smell the flowers" and enjoy the view.

Our hearts may be restless (because of the sweeping current that tumbles us along), but they are also sticky—like a hummingbird's tongue. We flit about in our present moment trying to find sweet nourishment, something to love and call our own. When we find such a lovely thing, some blossoming twig or other, we reach out to grasp it, hoping that it will hold us in place so that we can enjoy the delight of the present forever, trying to ignore the persistent pull of the current of time that calls us to move on.

There is nothing terribly wrong in taking time off to enjoy the present. Even the strongest ship must "lay to" every once in a while to take on supplies and get its bearings. The danger comes when we spend too long clutching our delightful twigs. We can become so entwined in our past and present that we turn our back on our future.

This would be a terrible mistake. Like it or not the Great Falls awaits us. We, like the rest of the human race, must someday plunge over the brink of this life into the "hidden places" beyond—a land (we are told) of quiet pools, brilliant rainbows, and soft refreshing mist.

Since this future is inevitable, how much better would it be for us to let go of our past and present, to stop fighting the current, and plunge towards our destiny with a laugh? But to do so we must be literally converted, turned around from the comforting bank, so that our attention is no longer captured, our hearts are no longer "stuck" to the pleasant twigs and blossoms of our present. These good things (our health, our strength, our possessions, our career, even our loves) are true goods, but they are no more stable than we. They too are swept along by time. It is therefore fantasy to believe that grasping them stops our movement towards the crashing Falls ahead. With them we are moving just as fast as before, it is just that for a brief period we move along together.

And so we must be converted, prepared to turn from both the good and bad in our present. Only then can we accept ourselves for what we truly are—little vessels floating temporarily on the stream of time until the day when, in accordance with God's providential plan, we too shall plunge over the Great Falls into a hidden place we cannot even imagine.

Faith tells us that there is "something" on the other side of our time here. Even in nature streams do not disappear once they plunge over a waterfall. Rather, they begin a new peaceful life of gentle movement into the endless ocean beyond.

And so it shall be for me, once I let go of the twigs that are holding me in place. The current of my time is rushing past. It is time for me to join it and see what world waits for me beyond the roar of the Great Falls.

## *Reflections of an Old Wise Man* 32

In the Scripture story of the Epiphany we are told that those mysterious wise men from the East found their God by following a star. But first they had to go looking for it.

The looking may have lasted for a long time but it did not lead immediately to action. Since they are called "wise men," I presumptively suggest that they were philosophers. If this presumption is true, then they most likely spent many years talking about what that star might be like—constructing and deconstructing the notion of "starity" *ad infinitum*— (in accord with the philosopher's claim: "I love wisdom; I could *talk* about it all day!"). No doubt they spent years spinning out exotic theories about what God might be like and about various ways of coming to that God. They talked and wrote and theorized and guessed but then, when the star finally *did* appear, they were challenged to get up off their hunches, climb on their camels, and follow that strange star into the darkness.

To their credit, they did just that. They did not let their pet convictions stand in the way of the facts—the fact that an unforeseen star had appeared and was calling them towards the unknown.

Now that I have come to age, I can see that such "star-searching" has been the story of my life and, indeed, is the story of every human life. The only difference between those Epiphany wise men and much of the rest of the human race is that they were willing to *look* for the star through a lifetime and were willing to follow it into strange places and then accept the unexpected that it revealed. For years they probably dreamed of finding a great philosopher king who would teach them the answers to all questions. Instead, they found a baby to be loved and in that love they found fulfillment of their life's search.

Sadly this does not happen in every human life. Some of us get tired of looking year after year, and we finally give up or settle for some lesser star. This is indeed too bad because we all need something that we can reach out for, something that will force us to extend ourselves, that will challenge us to leave our comfortable places and travel to lands we thought were far beyond us.

As an experiment, I once asked my students what three things they thought to be most important for happiness—what was the "star" that they were pursuing in life. Some said health (a foolish star for one who is necessarily falling apart); and some said enough money to insure security (a foolish star for one who someday will necessarily die); and some said love (which is not too foolish at all since love is a star that can lead even through sickness and death).

None of the things they mentioned were terribly bad. Indeed, all of them were good and desirable, but they were incomplete. Like so many stars that we "hitch our wagon to" in this life, my students' goals did not go far enough. What we humans really need is a "Messiah Star"—a light that will lead us into our future even when usual pleasures have dulled and earthly ambition is done and human loves have gone. We need such a star because we can lose all earthly goods if we live long enough.

When we finally come to age, it is then above all that we need a Messiah Star to lead us into the arms of our God. To realize *this* is at least the *beginning* of wisdom, and such a beginning is a true gift even for an old man. It is better to be an old wise man than never to be wise at all. It may just be the case that we will not begin to be wise until we are old. It may just happen that we will not even begin to follow our true star until we reach an age when any travel is difficult.

This should not surprise us. Getting old is a great incentive for humility, and some of us need to fall off our high horse before we can mount the camel that will take us in pursuit of our star.

*Seasons*                                           33

We witness the cycle of the seasons of the year many times. We go through the seasons of our life only once. As we pass through childhood and youth and middle age and old age, we see many springs and summers and autumns and winters. Augustine says we should look at yearly seasons and learn from them about the seasons of our lives (S 161, 10).

Any help I can get is much appreciated as I pass through the cycle of my life. Day follows night and night, day— shadow and light, light and shadow as year follows year. Spring green yields to summer rose and then to autumn gold and winter white as I spin through birth and youth and middle age and finally old age. I scale peaks and traverse valleys as I see years of seasons pass by, all the time gradually wearing out my life.

It always seemed strange to me that people would speak about the autumn of life, the golden years, as being the best of seasons. It is not so with the trees whose colors are the reason for calling the autumn "golden." For them their golden hues are a sign of ending, a going towards winter sleep. It is a time for losing past beauty. For some it is a time for being a bit nutty. The trees may look their prettiest in autumn, but in fact they are losing their moment in the sun. Their time for flourishing is over.

Still we celebrate their autumn as days of glory, because they look so fine and seem not to suffer in their decline. A tree with dying leaves does not remember its springtime and cannot foresee the winter cold that lies ahead. Indeed, if deciduous trees knew better, they would probably celebrate their temporary decline. Taking a long view, they seem to have a more exciting life than their cousins who change little from year to year. Perhaps that is why the weeping willow weeps. It has little variety in its life. What it is, it will be forever.

As for the evergreens, they have a particularly boring life. All geometric cones or spiky spines, they discourage affection. Their only hope for variety is to be brushed with winter snow or to be draped with tinsel and Christmas lights. Their humble virtue is in their ability to hold any decoration or bauble placed on their grasping foliage. If not glorious in themselves, they are at least receptive of any glory bestowed by some kind friend. Still they are "stand-offish": no place to hang a swing, dangerous to climb, impossible to hug, and deadly when eaten by the pet cat.

Humans, of course, are quite different from trees. In their late autumn days of age, they can *remember* and *foresee.* They can remember the flowers of their spring and the vigor of their summer. They can foresee what lies ahead . . . the dead of winter. In their autumn days humans can "feel" old, and that feeling makes the days seem less than perfect. Fearing the future, they are forced to look back to find the truly golden years. They look back nostalgically for the good old days and are unhappy.

It should not be so for a person who shares Augustine's faith. When he said that we should learn from the seasons of the year about our own lives, he meant it as a happy thought. If we look at the succession of seasons that have flowed through our years, we should know that winter is not the end of anything. It is just a resting period before a new and glorious spring. The message of the seasons and the message of Christianity is that indeed there *are* Golden Years, and they lie just ahead—even though we may now be in the autumn of our life.

## *Leaving Shadows*                                        34

Despite the number of my years, my shadow never ages. I may live through countless days and nights, but every morning's shadow is a new event untouched by my yesterday.

Now that I have come of age, my "yesterdays" are quite a few and my "tomorrows" are becoming less and less, but my shadow is indifferent to my changing times. It reflects my youth or my age without prejudice to either. Though I may be somewhat craggy now, my shadow has no wrinkles or scars, anymore than it had the brightness and smoothness of my childhood face. Indeed, a shadow is a poor indicator of the age of its master. The arthritic bend of age could just as well be the crouch of a young runner as far as a shadow is concerned. Of course, a shadow does reflect the girth and height of its source but fat or thin, tall or short, it cannot distinguish age and indeed, for those of us who have made a lifetime career of being "out-of-shape," it encompasses as much territory in old age as in the bloom of youth.

Our bodies cast shadows as long as we are erect. Our lives cast shadows as long as we are on this earth. These are the marks we make on the earth by our passing—the memories of us in the minds of those we have loved and who have loved us in return.

These shadows are ageless too. Once made, they cannot be changed or undone. They touch our loved ones long after we are gone—sometimes with as much pleasure or pain as they caused at their creation. Sometimes the shadows cast long ago are so powerful as to override any light or darkness we have brought to loved ones since. We are remembered more sometimes by the shadows of the past than by present presence. Thus, past cruelty will often sour recent kindness, and sometimes the shadow of a passionate love of long ago will "pleasure" one's life more than the polite friendship it has become. The paradox of shadows is indeed just this: sometimes "the way things were" leaves more potent shadows than "the way things are."

I remember going to a twenty-five-year reunion of a college class I taught as seniors. They said: "Why, you haven't changed a bit!" and I thought that either they were terribly near-sighted or were saying that I was an old fossil then as well as now. But then I came to realize that they were talking about my shadow—the memory of the good and bad we had shared so long ago. They were saying that our past together was more powerful than our fleeting, passing present.

My shadow will last, even as I do not, and perhaps that is the reason why, now that I am older, I seem to be more concerned about my shadow than my substance. I am less concerned about what I can accomplish here tomorrow than about what shadows my past life has cast on the lives of my loves. I am concerned about my "doings" tomorrow more for the shadows they create than the immediate matters of substance they accomplish.

I think now about the shadows I will leave behind when all my "todays" have become yesterday. When I die will I leave pleasant memories of a person good to know? Will I leave some ideas that might just give another hope or courage or happiness? Will my shadow leave a good taste in the mouth of the future? I hope my paranoia is not purely personal. I think it is not. All of us seem to have a desire to leave some mark on the earth before we leap into the heavens, a mark that will be recognized as ours and cherished as being something of value.

Now that I have come to age, I feel like I am in the midst of the last days of a long conference in a distant city. I am thinking of packing my bag and paying my bill. I am wondering what sort of TIP I should leave behind, some shadow that will mark the fact that I existed, some special piece of myself that will prevent me from simply sliding back into the anonymity of an unremembered face moving through an inn for transients.

Now that I am older, I am driven to make a good shadow in the lives of my loves, a shadow that will embrace and shade them as long as they live. Like the old Augustine, I don't want to "mess up" *now*, leaving behind a twisted ugly shadow of a life that became hurtful and wasted at the end. The days of my earthly future (good or bad) will pass as will all days, but the shadow that they cast will live forever in the hearts of my earthly loves and in the memory of my God.

Thus, now that I have come of age, I spread my heart and try even harder to cast good shadows on those I touch.

## *"Thanks for The Memories"* 35

Every experience, be it good or bad, sinks into our being and becomes part of our future. We are like sponges that absorb the loves and pains of the present, bringing them deep inside to be retained in our private quiet spaces.

When I find a love, that love comes into me and stays with me because it is now part of me. No matter how far away my loves are physically, they continue to rest in my heart and give me soft joy each day.

When I suffer hurt from a love, that hurt too is taken inside and lives there like the physical scars that remain on my skin after terrible physical wounds. My love-scar goes deep inside and becomes part of that great life-scar that comes from living for any time in an imperfect world. Hopefully my love-scar will not fester over time from my constant poking at it. I must try to leave such past wounds alone, letting them sink into the background of my life through my forgiveness. I probably can't get rid of it completely. It will always be there, painfully tender to the touch.

Happily the same persistence is characteristic of those loves that give me joy. I am never through with them. They may be far away but they are still with me. Knowing that they love me still, I feel their life inside me. I can reach inside and embrace them with my spirit at any time, even during my most public moments (which explains my sometime smile during solemn speeches). Certainly it would be just fine if they were here and available for a warm physical hug, but having their love and care over a distance is not bad. It is certainly better than having someone hold me who does not really "care a fig" for me.

And so, as I look back over my years I can fervently say to my lasting loves:

> Thanks for the memories! Our time together was brief but it gave me good memories to visit in the days ahead. Our days together were filled with words about life and death and love. They were days of problems solved, trials endured, simple pleasures, and good hope for fine days ahead. Through such memories you live in me each moment until fate or fortune or providence brings us together again. Till then I repeat again and again: "Thanks for the memories!"

## *Images of Life: The Golden Thread*　　36

Sometimes in class when I am trying to give an image of a human life, I will make a chalk-mark on the board no longer than my little finger and say: "Now this is the picture of my life from my beginning till now, my seventh decade."

The tiny finger of color that is my life now has some red for passion and orange for joy and green for hope and purple for sadness and black for despair. It has a bit of white for innocence and a lot of brown for repentance. Just now my life is mottled, neither completely good nor bad. It is a combination of many colors.

A blue stroke marks the end of this life in my drawing (blue has always been a restful color for me). This is my death, an event like any other event in this brief life except in this: after death there is a radical change in my existence. I symbolize this change by a line of purest yellow continuing across board after board until it disappears into infinity. The picture of my life now finished, I stand back and see that it is mostly this golden eternal thread which, once begun, will never end.

I make my eternal life gold because my faith tells me that whatever the joys of this life may have been, they are dark compared to blazing happiness of eternity. By comparison my life just now is dim and brief no matter how long I live. Looking at that tiny finger of mixed color that is "me" just now, I can see the truth of Augustine's saying that there is no such thing as a "long" life this side of death. Only eternal life is a long time because no life that ends in death can be called "long" (S 335B, 2).

And yet, my life just now is not inconsequential. It is here that I meet those loves with whom I shall share the rest of my eternal life. It is here that I get my first hint of that Divine Lover whom I shall see face to face in my golden days after death. It is here that I begin to experience the joy of knowing and the thrill of freedom—the joy that will cause me to cry "how wonderful" when I come to discover the mysteries of the eternal universe, the freedom by which I can "choose" and rejoice in the possession of the infinite good for whom I have been made.

Indeed, this little finger of time has eternal consequences. It determines the color of my life after death. Sad to say, a human life after death is not necessarily golden. I can color mine dark by the life I live now. In my present brief finger of life, I must have time for eternal concerns. I must open up the narrow space of my life so that the infinite can enter in. If I turn my back on that life now, the light will go out of my life after death.

My faith tells me that I must leave room in my life for God to touch me now. It tells me that if I do not consciously close God out of my little finger of time, God will give me a golden eternity. God's coming may not take away my troubles just now (my life may remain somewhat mottled), but it will prepare me for the golden days that can be my future.

The brevity of my life dictates that I must not waste it. At the same time I must not take it too seriously. I must not grasp at it as though it were indeed the "end all and be all" of my existence. I must not feel short-changed by a life that ends before others. I must not feel abused by a life that drags far beyond its prime. Long or short, any time is less than a blink in eternity's eye.

Thus, when I end here I am really just beginning. At death I will not have even *begun* to unravel the golden thread that is the rest of my life.

## *The Blind Lighthouse*  37

On the New Hampshire coast there is one of my very favorite houses, one which (things being different) I would have dearly loved to possess. At one time it had been a lighthouse, and for many years it had cast a piercing, saving beam far out over the brooding North Atlantic sea.

The enterprising family who had finally bought it and made it their home created in its tower the largest picture window I have ever seen. It is more that two stories tall and faces towards the ocean. When in the morning I rode past on the coastal road, I could sometimes see folks enjoying their coffee as they watched the rising sun. Passing by at night, the road would be ablaze with a shower of light from the massive window, testifying to the existence of happy life on an otherwise dreary shore. I never had coffee there myself nor was I ever invited to the parties (they had no need for a philosopher, I guess), but in my dreams I spent many hours standing at that window looking out over the constantly changing sea.

No wonder that I was saddened when, on a recent visit, I found my dream house all boarded up. My poor lighthouse had become blind. No longer was it able to see the glorious light of God's dawn. No longer was it a beacon of hope and joy for those passing on the dark shore road and the sea beyond. Its light had gone out, and what remained was no more than a shell, a temporary rest for pilgrim birds. If there was still light inside, no one outside could see it. As far as the world could know, its days of being a comfort for those without and a place of joy for those within were over. It was empty, all life long departed for sunnier climes.

Looking at my blind lighthouse, I wondered if that was what would happen to me as more and more I come to age. Now in my seventh decade it *does* seem that my days of casting dramatic light on a world at sea are mostly over. My light has dimmed. Most of what I have had to say has been said. Most of what I might have been, has been. My mark on life is not so much my future promise or my present work as it is my history. I live not in hope for new loves, but in the enjoyment and remembrance of loves long treasured. I live more and more within myself and the light still shining in my craggy hulk becomes less and less apparent to those passing by.

But perhaps this is not a sad event. Perhaps it is proper for an aging lighthouse and an aging man to spend more time inside themselves reflecting on life and love and days past. There may even be great light and warmth in so living. After all, a house that is boarded up against the violent changing winds and has its curtains drawn against the gathering cold may still be warm and bright inside if its occupant has had the sense to gather fuel to support life when the world outside begins to dim. If I store up precious memories and dear loves deep in my heart as I go through life, it is just possible that even an ordinary fellow like me can peacefully endure the dimming light of that world beyond my fleshy shell when the time comes for me to feel my age.

If Augustine is right that the place of the Divine is not outside but inside the human person, then there is just the chance that when my house is gradually boarded up by increasing age, this will not be a sign of dying but of finding new life. My frame may have become quite gnarled and my windows may seem dark, but inside I can be filled with a new light. Indeed, with my windows to the world mostly covered over, I may for the first time be free of the distractions of my "salad days," those whirling lights and noisy parties that prevented me from feeling the fire of God within. When I finally "come of age" and my little house is closed off from much of the world, I may actually be quite happy inside, basking in that Divine Light that I came to see only after I had boarded up my windows and sat down quietly deep inside myself, waiting patiently for what the future had in store.

## *Thoughts at Sunset*                               38

Sometimes in the evening of a day there comes a glorious sunset. Of course, the sun sets on every day and on every life, but on some special days the sun seems to almost "plunge" below the horizon, leaving at the very end a burst of light on the darkening land of the day that has just past.

As an old photographer I can testify to the fact that the colors change quickly. Sometimes I have gone through a whole roll of film in two or three minutes trying to capture the changing colors. Each new sunset second is different, an explosion of color that literally shows this old world in a new light. Watching it for the first time, it is hard to decide which moment is the most glorious. You need to process the film to see what will develop. When finally you hold the frozen memories in your hands, sometimes you find a special moment that you will treasure for all time.

Looking out at a sunset is something like looking back through the day of my life. The clouds and dust that are residues of my past add to the beauty, serving as prisms that bend and mold the harsh white light of time into the colors of my days. The evening clouds are like my dreams, billowing to the heavens in multiple shapes—castles and ice cream cones, dark memories of storms endured, pink prophecies of future glory.

A sunset seems to enhance your past. Children or grandchildren that stand with you cast long shadows—promises of great things to come for the family you have created. As you wait for your sun to set, you look behind you at your past and wonder that the harsh wounding waves of past passion seem softened, while remembered joys stand out like tiny boats aglow with their own light far out on a darkening sea.

If one shares one's sunset with a loved one, it is even better. Embracing as your sun sets, the shadow of your love seems to cover the whole world behind—the hills and valleys of your past. All seem to lose importance in the great shadow of your lasting love and the glorious light that lies before you. There is no better way to see your sunset than to see it reflected in the eyes of one who loves you.

We should learn from our lives that a gray morning haze

is no prediction that our day will not be sunny. Foggy morn-
ings sometimes precede blazingly bright noons. So too the
dimming powers of our "greying" years give no hint of the
sunshine and bright colors that lie just a bit ahead.

They say that it is the darkest before the dawn. Perhaps
it will only be after death that we will realize that the end
of our lives was not the dusk of a dimming sun presaging
the dark of a starless night. Rather, it was more like God
coming and putting out a flickering lamp because God knew
that the dawn had come.

## *Gambling on a Dream*   39

When I was somewhat younger, someone much older
wondered aloud to me why it was that the elderly seemed
to have more dreams. Now that I too have come of age,
I can see what he meant. My night dreaming now is not
filled with one great dramatic epic. Rather it is a series of
selected shorts—sometimes cartoons, sometimes newsreels
of worlds that never happened, never *previews* of coming
attractions but frequent *reviews* of the past shows of my life.

Of course, part of the change in the character of my
dreams comes from a change in the character of my sleeping. I sleep in fits and starts. Eight hours of uninterrupted
sleep seems to escape me now. My nights are now spent in
many comings and goings. Each night a different part of
my body takes its turn resting fitfully, demanding attention
after a few hours, forcing the rest of us to get up and comfort it in its distress. If dreams are the doors through which
we enter and exit deep sleep, it is no wonder that I dream
more.

I have noticed that now most of my dreams are made
up of past events, more often than not changed in some odd,

unpredictable way. Dreams never seem to match reality. Sometimes my dreams are very much better. In my sleep I sometimes make worlds of "what might have been" into fantastic worlds of "what *is*," and I wake with reluctance and sadness to the reality of my life. But sometimes my reality is better than any dream—unexpected victories, disasters avoided by chance, loves enjoyed that I could never *dream* of having. At times my dreams are nightmares and I wake sweating and shaking, glad to be back to a modestly pleasant world where my worst fears have not been realized. Be they good or bad, I cannot live with my dreams for very long. My dreams can embellish my life but they cannot change the reality that defines it.

Of course, dreams are not restricted to the elderly. We dream at every age. While the old may dream through the night about the past, the young daydream about the future. When I was little, I dreamed of being noble and grand when I grew up. "When I grow up (I dreamed), I will never be stupid or silly. I will never hurt those that I love and I will conquer any pain that comes my way by a simple act of my decisive will." When maturity finally arrived, I discovered that I was not a king after all and began to dream in a new way, at a lower level of expectation. I dreamed of being "not *too* silly" and being able to say "I'm sorry" and being able to endure the pain that I could not change.

Like the rest of humanity, I spend much of my life, even now, gambling on dreams. There is nothing especially wrong with that. Indeed, it is through my dreams that I can touch infinity. In my dreams I move beyond the static "actual" and the safe "probable" to every "possible" worth seeking. In reaching for such possibilities, I become larger than my life. Even though my dream may never come true, I am better for having had it.

But sometimes I *do* go off the deep end in my dreaming. A short time ago I joined millions and millions of others in gambling on a dream, the dream of winning the state lot-

tery (at the time worth $80,000,000). I gambled on a dream
and for a while was happy in my hope. No matter that the
odds of my winning were one in ten million. No matter that
it was more likely that I would be hit by lightning than win,
no matter that it was more likely that I would *die* on Wednesday than that my ticket would win on Wednesday. I did
not care about my odds, for I had my dreams—dreams of
what I would do with the money if I won.

I did not know *if* I would win, but I knew exactly *how*
I would use my winnings:

- I would give up philosophy and study sociology since
  sociologists seem to have more fun.
- I would give up wearing hats and buy some hair so that
  I could be handsome.
- I would give up being old and buy back thirty years of
  life and live my days as a healthy youth.
- I would give up being lonely and go to some store and
  buy someone to love me.

My dreams were silly but no more silly than the belief
that academic degrees bring happiness, or that beauty rests
on appearances, or that time can be reversed, or that love
can be bought.

I and my fellow gamblers lined up on Wednesday to buy
our chances, and we were happy for a while sharing a common dream. Waiting to take our chance, our possible winnings became almost tangible. The enthusiasm of other
dreamers made each feel a part of something truly important. We were a community dedicated to a common goal:
a better life where everything would be just fine forever.

When Thursday came it was clear that the dream had
ended. Most of us had lost. Our dream was over and we
went our separate ways to pursue dreams that we shared
with no one else. We had lost the lottery and had to find
personal salvation in some other way.

As a Christian who has come of age, I am now left
mostly with the promises of Christ as a guarantee for a fine

future. Realistically, there is not too much time to realize temporal dreams. My future now is mostly beyond time and demands a more radical gamble: a gamble that the Christian message is indeed true:

- that indeed I live in a world controlled by God,
- that indeed I shall live forever,
- that indeed my ultimate happiness is (with God's grace) placed squarely in my hands.

Given the truth of that message, my dream of winning heaven is a well-founded hope. Indeed, the odds are three to one in favor: the love from the Father, salvation by the Son, and guidance of the Holy Spirit versus my own sometime perversity.

The rewards for such a realized dream are just fine too:

- feeling good forever;
- being young forever;
- having love forever.

Considering the odds and the rewards, it is not a bad dream to gamble on—even for an old fossil.

## *Eagle Wings*     40

Now that I have come to age, I perceive that my physical strength is lessening. It is not quite so easy to walk any more, much less run. Muscles have grown weak, and there is no exercise regime that will bring back their twenty-year-old vigor. It seems more difficult to control the quality and quantity of my body: memory, sight, breath, breadth, and more humble processes all seem somewhat out of control.

Of course, my spirit is always brand new. Souls never grow up or grow old, but they do seem to be affected by their environment, and my old neighborhood has definitely gone down hill. My soul is now living in an aging building, one where the windows are fogged over and the plumbing does not always work and the exterior could stand some new siding. My spirit may be just fine in its power (if not its direction), but it is lessened in the exercise of those activities that depend on its fossilizing friend, my body. I may be able with the best of the young to raise my arms to heaven and cry "Praise God!" But I cannot avoid the twinge of shoulder bursitis coming from such imprudent ecstasy.

My life seems to be characterized by a continuing process of "giving up" painful physical activity. In my twenties I gave up basketball (the leaping was still fine but the landing was agony). In my thirties I gave up playing five sets of tennis singles in one day (finding it took three days to recover). In my forties I gave up jogging (I could still run three miles but I could not climb stairs afterwards). In my fifties I gave up golf (for mental rather than physical reasons). Now that I am in my sixties I am reduced to power-lurching down college paths, driven by the principle, "Move it or lose it!" I know I am not as bad off as I could be (and I thank God for that), but I also am fairly sure that I am not as bad as I will be.

In sum, I seem to be falling apart—now that I have come to age. I am reaching the end of that great battle between anabolism and catabolism that began at my conception and will end at my death (DCD, 13.10). Each day I suffered a "little death" in my sleep, preparing me for that "great sleep" that will be my death (S 221, 3). Indeed my growing feebleness is but the extension of my future death into my present life (ENN 84, 10). There is nothing in my life now that was not present long ago. My sleeping and my changing was present as much in my youth as in my age, but then I did not think about it. I was too much involved in jumping for rebounds, rushing the net, running in circles, and mulling over "unlieable plays."

Augustine remarked once that our lives are really nothing more than a song of which death is the last note (DVR 22.42). Now that I have come to an age when I must "face the music," it is comforting to realize that this life now is but the first movement in a great symphony where the second movement will go on forever, a sublime music that I can hear even now sounding deep inside my spirit (ENN 42, 7).

No matter how decrepit or out of breath I may feel just now, the great prophecy of Isaiah will come true for me too:

> Though young men faint and grow weary,
>   and youths stagger and fall,
> They that hope in the LORD will renew their strength,
>   they will soar as with eagle's wings;
> They will run and not grow weary,
>   walk and not grow faint.
>
> Isa 40: 30-31

Perhaps that is implied too in the promise Jesus made: "Come to me all you who are weary and find life burdensome, and I will refresh you . . . Your souls will find rest" (Matt 11: 28-29).

He certainly does not mean that he will make me feel all that better just now. That is for my future. But perhaps the pain I sometimes feel in my shoulders means that he has already begun the process of fitting me with those wings that are to carry me to eternity and through eternity, those wings that will enable me to fly higher than I could ever jump and faster than I could ever run.

## Epilogue: "We'll Meet Again . . ."

At the end of growing older is being young: so my mentor Augustine assures me. Having walked through this life to an advanced age, I shall finally die and then, after a period of rest, my soul shall be reunited with my resurrected body, and I shall feel fine forever. I will be forever young, in the prime of my life (DCD, 22.20). It is a refreshing thought as I twist and turn in my seat seeking relief from aching legs, trying to find the appropriate lens in my trifocals to see the words I have written.

When my days of being old are finished, I need no longer worry about "another tying me fast and carrying me off against my will" (John 21:18). I will no longer be bounded or in bonds to my past nor the maladies of age. I shall be free. I shall be young. I shall be friends with my body (S 155, 14.15).

At the end of aging, there will be a parting and that will be somewhat sad. It will be something like the "leaving of the Lord" at Emmaus (Luke 24:31). After walking with his two friends through a day and sharing an evening meal with them, Jesus got up to go. The gospel story does not record any parting words but, for reasons hidden deep in my feverish old mind, I can imagine him singing to his saddened friends the words of that old song:

> We'll meet again.
> Don't know where; don't know when.
> But I know we'll meet again
> Some sunny day.

Now that I have come of age, I can see that my whole life is much like that one day on the road to Emmaus. I began my trek alone, with no past, no goals, no understanding of the life that I was to live. But as my life went on, I was soon joined by others: strangers who became family and friends through conversation, sharing hopes and opinions and dreams about the meaning of life and where it was leading. Starting alone, I found strangers and made them loves by giving them a piece of my time, a portion of my heart. We became intimates. They came into my little place and into my very being, so that it seemed that we became one: two solitary cells coming together to form a home.

In them and in me Jesus truly walked. Seeing our love, he joined us on the road and walked with us through all of our days, even though we did not always recognize him for what he was. He talked with us and in us about the meaning of life and what the future would be like. He forgave us the past and told us not to worry. He promised that he would be there at the end of the day if only we invite him to stay with us.

Death often comes as a surprise, no matter how long we live. And thus it may happen for me that I won't notice that my day is coming to a close until the darkness closes in around me. I will sit for one last meal with those loves and that God who have walked with me through life. Then he will get up to leave (as he did at Emmaus so long ago), this time taking my hand to go with him. I will rise (perhaps stiffly after my long walk through life) and go with him into the evening that precedes the new dawn.

And who knows? Perhaps I will have time to look back at my friends who are still in their years of coming of age and join with Jesus in singing to them his great song of leaving—the Emmaus song:

We'll meet again.
Don't know where; don't know when.
But I *know* we'll meet again
Some sunny day.